# 88 UNASHAMED BLACK MENTAL HEALTH STORIES

## A BLACKLANDIA ANTHOLOGY

88 Unashamed Black Mental Health Stories: A Blacklandia Anthology

ISBN: 978-1-7344977-2-4



Permissions
Inlandia Institute
Executive Director: Mckenna Deluca-Martinez
4076 Brockton Avenue
Riverside, CA 92501

Book Layout & Design: Kirk Visola
Cover Artist: Kirk Visola
Editor: Romaine Washington
Assistant Editor: Marcus Muscato

Printed and bound in the United States
Distributed by Ingram

Published by Inlandia Institute
Riverside, California
www.InlandiaInstitute.org

# Contents

**MIND AND BODY WISDOM**



**LIVING IN BLACK SKIN**

## ABUSE AND RESILIENCE



## DIAGNOSED BUT NOT DEFINED BY MY CONDITION

**WE ARE A QUILT**



**VOICE FOR THE VOICELESS**

**INTERNAL STRUGGLE TO LIVE**

# Introduction

Taraji P. Henson, Simone Biles, and Trevor Noah have openly talked about their challenges with depression. Many of us assume that if we have a successful career, financial stability, and good friends, we will be happy. These admired celebrities dispel the myth that mental wellness is about accomplishments and prosperity. We learn from them that it is ok to be vulnerable and ask for help, and it is essential to advocate for ourselves. However, even with notable Black celebrities and athletes speaking out, there are ingrained cultural habits of denial, rooted in fear and stigma that prevent so many from getting the help we need.

Denial is one of our greatest enemies because it masquerades as strength. You don't admit when you are sick, physically, emotionally, or mentally. It is not unusual for us to dismiss peculiar behavior and ignore or monitor menacing outbursts. You might hear someone say, "You know how he is," or "Don't pay her no mind," or "They'll be alright, just leave them alone for a while." Some of us develop effective coping strategies, and others persevere, self-medicate with food or other substances and activities.

A concerned person might ask, "Why don't you go to the doctor?" The response, "You can't trust them." Denial has taken the form of the insistent mantra of "no labels," even in the face of obvious symptoms. "I won't have them give my child or me a label. Those things follow you for life and close doors and opportunities."

However, there are valid reasons for skepticism. Some of the fear and denial of the need for help is rooted in the biases in psychiatry and medical institutions. As far back as 1851, Dr. Samuel A. Cartwright used pseudoscience to create the term drapetomania, a supposed "illness" of which the only symptom was a Black enslaved person's desire to run away from their master. Cartwright also created the term dysaethesia aethiopicatoan, another supposed "illness" which caused Black enslaved people to be lethargic or lazy. The prescribed cure for both of these conditions was torture and beatings.

In *The Protest Psychosis: How Schizophrenia Became a Black Disease*, author Jonathan Metzyl details the nefarious way by which many Black people, who were fighting for equality in the 60s and 70s, were arrested and labeled as violent schizophrenics. They were warehoused and brutalized in asylums. The response to this travesty was to drastically overhaul the mental health care system. Facilities were closed, and funding was cut.

Trust is earned in increments. Despite the not-too-distant past abuses, at present, there is a dire need for mental health advocacy in the Black community. According to a thirteen-year study (2007-2020) by the Pew Charitable Trust, the suicide rate rose 144% among Black children ages ten to seventeen. Honest conversations about mental health care are crucial in the Black community.

Imagine reading a short story, a poem, an essay, or viewing artwork that speaks to you about a struggle you wrestle with in secret. The reason you don't share your very private experience is shame. You feel like you should be stronger; you shouldn't be going through this.

Perhaps it is not you, maybe it is a loved one, a friend, or your child. Questions harass you. What did you do wrong to allow this to happen? What could you have done differently? Is there a way to make it go away without anyone knowing?

Just knowing there is someone else who has had a similar experience and feels free enough to use their craft to breathe truth and light into confusion and pain can be a great comfort. Stigma begins to dissolve. Each time you read or hear about someone who has had a similar struggle, the more you realize the secret will not devour you, and maybe it doesn't need to be hidden.

You begin to wonder what it would feel like to own it and speak up about it. The cloak of shame gets lighter and lighter until truth lifts it completely and makes healing out loud an option. I am grateful to the Black creative counselors, psychologists, social workers, psychiatrists, and members of the National Alliance on Mental Illness (NAMI) whose contributions to this collection provide 88 Black mental health stories. The various works are listed under categories.

In **FAMILY DYNAMICS**, authors examine the expectations, frustrations, and hopes in familial relationships. **FAITH AND MENTAL HEALTH** authors reveal the struggle to find balance between faith and the need for professional mental health when necessary. In **MIND AND BODY WISDOM**, the connection between physical well-being and mental health is explored through essays and poetry, while **LIVING IN BLACK SKIN** exposes the emotional impact of the alienating, brutal history of slavery and institutional racism. A sonnet, the blues, and even humor will surprise you as various forms of abuse and resilience are explored in the section on **ABUSE AND RESILIENCE**. In **DIAGNOSIS DOES NOT DEFINE ME** two members from the mental health community share their portraits, names, and diagnoses in the hopes of continuing to break the stigma associated with mental illness. **WE ARE A QUILT** in this tapestry of candid, poetic descriptions of living with different diagnoses; we gain insight and compassion. In **VOICE FOR THE VOICELESS**, there is a deep vein of empathy running through these writers who give voice to those we seldom acknowledge or hear. We briefly visit their trauma and isolation; here, their voices have profound value. In **INTERNAL STRUGGLE FOR LIFE**, the readers are taken on a journey from suicidal ideation to embracing life despite disappointments and hardships; we are encouraged to reframe ourselves in a vibrant future of hope.

Discussion questions are at the end of each section to spark reflection and conversation. There is also information on five topics listed here along with their page numbers: *Mental Health Check-ups* (55), *Racism* and *Post-Traumatic Stress Disorder* (95), *Attention-Deficit/Hyperactivity Disorder* (152), *Cutting* and *Non-Suicidal Self-Injury* (179), and *Depression and Suicide* (209).

By Romaine Washington, Editor

Shame is not your name. Shame is not my name.
There is nothing wrong with you. There is nothing wrong with me.
We have patterns to unlearn, new behaviors to embody, and wounds to heal.
But there is nothing wrong with us and the core of who we are.
We are unlearning generations of shame and remembering love.
It takes time. And the time is now.

–Yolo Akili Robinson,
Founder and Executive Director of
Black Emotional and Mental Health Collective

# Family Dynamics

I've learned that people will forget what you said,
people will forget what you did,
but people will never forget how you made them feel.

—Maya Angelou

# The Mushroom Garden

by Justin C. Key

"Austin, watch after your brother," Dad said to me. "Joey, be good."

Dad didn't wait for a response. He pushed our shopping cart to the side and went to exchange a carton of milk for one that wasn't lactose-free. Dad left us alone in situations like this more and more. He fought with Mom about it. That us boys needed to learn independence. Maybe if they stopped coddling us, we'd grow up and out of whatever phase this was. Mom thought we needed more, not less. I didn't know. Maybe we would grow out of it. Maybe Dad just didn't want the bother.

I suddenly felt alone in the large Brooklyn grocery store and joined Joey by the aisle to see what he had an eye for. My little brother was good at finding interesting things.

"What are you looking at, Joey?" I asked. Joey was five years old and had never answered a single question. At least, not in the way people expected. Still, I asked them like I would ask anyone else. Mom did, too. The rare times Dad did, the question was covered in a flavor that said Joey would never really get it. That Joey was different. I didn't like that word, or any of its ideas. Different. Special was much better. The way Mom said it, in that proud, accomplished sort of way.

Joey stood still, his eyes fixed on the shelves of arugula, green peppers, and baby lettuce. His lips were a straight line under his nose, like a puppet's. I placed my ear to his and saw what Joey saw.

Grow Your Own Mushroom Garden, the box said. It was tucked between packages of neatly cut Portobello and a bucket of Shitake twined together like jungle vines. The box was paper-bag brown and the size of a milk carton. In bold letters on the top were the words, "Just add water and watch it grow! Fun for Kids!"

I looked around. The grocery store was alive with people, and the space loud with boops and the exchange of goods between carts, hands, and conveyor belts. I scanned for a wide-shouldered man with more hair on his chin than his head, and whose right shoulder dipped when he walked. I didn't see Dad.

"This looks f-f-f-un, huh Joey?" I whispered the word 'fun' a few times. The speech therapist I talked to through the computer screen said, 'practice, practice, practice.'

My focused brother traced the box's lettering with his finger. He mouthed words that didn't seem to be there, but I knew better. They had to be there. The way Joey saw things was special. I often wished I could see what Joey saw.

Joey grabbed a bag of baby lettuce and put it over the row of boxes. Then he took it away, put it back, and took it away again. He repeated this peek-a-boo routine several times. Nerves grew fingers around me. Dad would be back soon. He didn't like Joey's routines. And he really didn't like wasting money. Would he see a box of dirt as a waste? Probably. From what Dad told Mom, there wasn't much left after 'all that the boys need'.

The routine done, Joey walked away from the veggies section of the produce aisle and crawled into the bottom of the shopping cart. That space used to be for packages of paper towels and bottles of water. Now it was for Joey.

I checked again for Dad. The coast was clear, I grabbed the mushroom box and stuffed it in the cart. With its brown cardboard and faint lettering, it was easy to notice. I moved it underneath a loaf of organic bread and a bag of rice.

"What are you messing with, Austin?" came Dad's voice. His hand gripped my arm and pulled it out of the cart. "You're going to mash the bread. I need you to be a slow engine."

'Slow engine' meant bringing things to a crawl, like Thomas the Train. "I-I-I . . ."

Dad cut me off. "'Yes, Dad.' No excuses."

"Yes, Dad." Dad let go of my arm. The slight indentation didn't hurt. The mushroom garden went unnoticed.

Dad softened as we found an open cashier. "You know I'm just trying to teach y'all right, now, don't you, son?"

I nodded and held my breath as I helped unload the basket. Would Dad see the garden?

"Come on out, Joey." Dad dipped his head under the cart. "It's time to go. Don't you want to help your dad pay?"

Joey ran his fingers over an invisible chalkboard. "Portobello," he said.

"Joey, it's time to go, so come on—"

"Portobello, Portobello, Portobello!"

I snuck the mushroom garden onto the conveyor belt and knelt down on the other side of the cart. I crawled forward, touched Joey's hand, and opened my mouth to start Mom's calming mantra. Dad's sharp voice made me start.

"I got it, Austin!"

The tired look in Dad's eyes spread. What was left of his smile went away. I often dreamed of him walking away after trying and failing to connect with Joey and never coming back. Moments like this made me fear my dream would come true. Dad stood up. I scrambled to cover the now-moving garden with a bag of flour tortillas. I wasn't fast enough.

Dad picked up the box and turned it like an alien artifact. He mouthed the words, eyed Joey, shook his head, and handed it to the cashier.

"We won't be getting this."

Joey let out a wail. "Portobello!" Dad winced. He caught my stare and the cashier's worried look. Our father's jaw tightened. He bent forward and pulled Joey out, kicking and screaming. He got my brother under one arm. Dad was meaty and strong and had done this many times. But Joey, like me, was growing. For the first time, Dad struggled.

"Portobello! Portobello!"

"Focus on the groceries, Austin," Dad said, stern and direct. I picked up the pace. Then, to the cashier, "You good?"

The cashier lowered his gaze. "You, uh, want bags?"

"Yes. Please. Thanks."

As my father wrestled with Joey and the cashier scrambled for bags, a strange, exciting, thoughtless urge came over me. I lunged forward, my feet coming clean off the floor, grabbed the mushroom garden from behind the register, and threw it back on the conveyor belt.

The cashier saw. We locked eyes. He gave a half grin and rang up my secret. Dad hardly looked at the checkout screen as he swiped a shiny card.

Dad carried Joey all the way out to the car while I pushed the heavy cart of bagged groceries. Joey stopped screaming for portobello and yelled for Mom. I waited for this fire to ignite Dad's fury, usually an eerie silence that sucked the fun out of the air. But as he loaded my little brother into the back seat and secured his seatbelt, mostly Dad just looked tired.

•••

Mom worked as a waitress at a small Italian restaurant on the other side of Brooklyn. I learned a lot from the words that drifted around the dark, third-story apartment during their late-night bedroom talks. Mom had taken a 'break' from nursing school when I was born, and that 'break' became a 'sacrifice' when Joey arrived. It costs a lot of money to become a nurse.

Mom stood out in the building's hallway as we came up the stairs. Joey was still slung over Dad's shoulder.

"We're late for Joey's session," Mom said. She touched my head as I hugged her.

"Good to see you, too, Dee," Dad said. "I thought that was yesterday."

"Yesterday was occupational therapy. Today is speech. It's on the calendar."

Dad muttered something about the calendar as he dropped the grocery bags in the kitchen and then lowered my brother onto the linoleum. Joey tried to make a beeline for the bags, but Mom shuttled him to the living room where the virtual therapist waited on her laptop screen.

"I got it, Joey," I whispered and squeezed his hand. There was a beat of calm, and for a moment I thought maybe my brother understood me.

"What was that, Austin?" Dad was already putting the groceries away.

"Can I help?" I said.

"Always. After, we can run some drills. Your games start up next week. I think this league will be more your speed." Dad cocked his head. "You think Joey can play?"

I didn't like sports. They were boring to watch and scary to play. The other kids were so hungry to score, no matter what. I avoided getting hurt, no matter what. Everyone got so mad when I let the soccer ball roll by, or I covered my head under the rim instead of jumping for the rebound. Dad loved basketball. It brought out his rare joy. At first, I expected him to yell at me like he yelled at the players on TV. But Dad beamed whenever I so much as breathed on the ball during a game. I liked that feeling. I wished I could like it more than I feared everything else.

But Joey? He'd spend the entire game counting the bumps on the basketball.

"I'll try," I said. Dad liked a trier.

There. Finally. I pulled the brown box from the grocery bag while Dad faced the fridge. Operating on that same energy that had overtaken me at the store, I ran out of the kitchen, into our room, and hid it under the bed I shared with Joey.

Dad was waiting when I returned.

"You know I don't like you sneaking food. We only eat at the kitchen table."

"Yes, Dad."

Dad lifted an eyebrow. I went back to the room and found an unopened bag of cheddar popcorn. Would Dad remember that we hadn't actually gotten popcorn? Or that popcorn was Joey's favorite, not mine? These thoughts plucked the nerves still wrapped around me. Maybe it would be easier to just hand over the garden.

But Dad was on the phone when I came back into the kitchen.

"I need proof. He's worked at the shop for years, way before I took it over. I've never known him to steal. I know. I know. Show me the receipts, and I'll deal with it."

When Dad saw me, he held out his hand. I gave him the popcorn. He shook his head, dipped the phone, mouthed to me, 'no eating in the bedroom,' gave me a quick side hug, and sent me to go play with my brother.

• • •

I knew fear. I just couldn't explain it. What would happen if Dad found out about the garden? Would he 'spank' us? He never had, even though his own 'Mom used to wear his ass out.' Would he leave, like in my dreams, like his father left him? My first-grade teacher the year before said some dreams come true. She'd said it with hope. Her words gave me dread.

Joey worried in his own way. He 'stimmed' more, a word Mom used for when Joey bird-flapped his arms or made frog-like noises with his throat. While Dad tried to show us how to dribble, Joey created a completely new stim: he pumped the basketball between his hands really fast, like he was charging it up. With my clumsiness and Joey's wandering attention, Dad was already frustrated. He didn't like this at all.

"Stop it, Joey," he said. A vein came down his wrinkled forehead, a faint lightning bolt drawn on lined paper. "Joey. Joey!"

Dad knocked the ball out of Joey's hand hard enough for it to bounce over the living room table and break the lamp. Mom came out of the bedroom, yelling Then Dad yelled. I cried. Joey stimmed. With no ball to pump, he pushed his palms against his own temples. Terrified, I tried to stop him. Mom stopped me.

"Leave him, Austin," Mom said. She punched numbers into her phone. "Let him regulate."

"Who you calling?" Dad said.

But Mom was already on it. Soon, a woman's voice calmly told them to go into another room, away from the kids. I controlled my sobs and listened through the door. The voice sounded like the woman Mom and Dad usually met through the computer, the woman who helped them 'work better as a team.'

Half of what the woman said was muffled. Then, Dad's voice, loud and sharp. "A date? That's what you recommend?"

That night, Marcella came.

Babysitters didn't go well. Mom and Dad usually came home early, flustered, with the babysitter already waiting by the door. Marcella, the only one who could 'handle' us, had a kindness that tasted fake. I could tell Mom didn't like her, either.

Mom and Dad dressed up nice, and they smelled good. Still, there was an unspoken heat between them.

Dad pulled me aside. "Be good. You're man of the house tonight." He hugged me. We both liked hugs. I wished Joey liked hugs. When Dad tried to hug him, my brother squirmed away as if Dad smelled like beans.

Marcella's fake kindness left with our parents. She went to scroll through her phone from the couch and scolded me whenever I let Joey out of my sight.

"What's that?" Marcella asked when she saw us take the mushroom garden to the kitchen. She was older than Mom, with hair dyed so black it looked plastic.

"It-it-it-it," I began. I licked my lips. "S-sorry."

Marcella waved away my apology. "What is that?" she repeated.

"It-it's a garden," I said. "A m-mushroom garden. We're planting it."

"Oh, a toy," Marcella said. "Don't make a mess."

I placed the box on top of the kitchen counter. Inside was a plastic bag stuffed with what looked like chocolate-chip ice cream, a small spray bottle, and a single white sheet of paper.

I read over the instructions: expose the bag, cut a couple of slits in it, keep it wet, and watch it grow! I whispered the words most likely to trip up my tongue and then read them out loud to Joey.

"I think you'll like this," I said.

"Open the front panel and cut a plus sign in the soil bag," Joey said. It was the first line of the instructions, word-for-word.

"That's right, Joey," I said. "Then we have to—"

"Open the front panel and cut a plus sign in the soil bag." Joey carefully peeled off the front panel, creating a hole in the middle of the empty box. He repeated his new phrase three times. He picked up the bag of dirt and put it back in the box. The yellow and white-stained soil could be seen through the new hole, like an exposed plastic belly.

Joey traced the length of the plastic and then across it. He did this over and over. Joey's finger started and ended at the same exact place each time and stayed straight throughout. I tried to copy the motion on the off-white carpet. Good, but not as good as Joey's.

"Open the front panel and cut a plus sign in the soil bag. Open the front panel and cut a plus sign in the soil bag."

"Maybe I should do it," I said.

"Open the front panel and cut a plus sign in the soil bag."

Only a counter separated the kitchen from the living room. Marcella glanced over but said nothing. She expected me to handle my brother.

You're man of the house tonight.

"Okay, okay, Joey. Sheesh."

I found a steak knife in the kitchen drawer, hesitated, and then held it out. Joey immediately took it. My heart leapt from my imagination's quick painting of all kinds of horror.

Joey pressed the knife's sharp edge to the plastic. It dipped into the chocolate chip soil; Joey unzipped the undeveloped garden like a jacket. He stopped just short of the other end and then did the same horizontally, forming the plus sign described in the instructions.

I feared Joey would fall into one of his routines, carving the sign over and over again until the one mushroom garden became four. I was ready to grab the knife right after the initial cut, but Joey surprised me by putting it to the side. The cut was perfect.

"Place the bag away from sunlight. Place the bag away from sunlight."

Joey set the garden down, picked up the spray bottle, and walked over to the sink. He filled the bottle and tested the spray on his own tongue. My brother looked at me, smacked his lips, and gave a smile as big as Marcella's, only Joey's didn't remind me of clowns.

Joey placed the finished garden on the windowsill. Our apartment faced another building, and the sun only reached the window for a few minutes in the evening. Joey squinted as the streetlight's lemon glow hit his face. Joey didn't slow or falter. Joey was focused. He sprayed the opening in the box four times. Only four, just like the instructions said.

When a routine did come, I was almost relieved. Joey, without routine, was like a playground without a slide, a fish tank without any fish. He nudged one side of the box and watched how the light hit the soil's different grooves. He nudged it the other way, pushed it forward, pulled it back. I watched with fascination.

Sometime later, Mom and Dad's laughter drifted from the hallway and died outside our door. Marcella shot up and went to fake babysit Joey, who was still by the mushroom garden. Mom came right over; her eyes were drawn to the box.

"What's this?" she said. And then, to Marcella, "Is it yours?"

I mentally pleaded for Marcella to say that it was. For her to prove more useful than just a warm, adult body to 'watch' us.

"Definitely not," Marcella said. "They set it up when you left."

Useless.

"I-I-I . . ." I started.

"Slow engine," Mom said. "You're not in trouble."

Yet. I licked my lips. "I got it-it from the gro-grocery store for Joey. I forgot to tell Dad."

"I'm sure it's fine."

"No! He-he didn't wan-want me to-to—"

Mom touched my head and glanced over at Dad, who was putting away the pizza boxes from dinner. "Everything okay?" he said.

"Everything's fine," Mom said. She tilted her chin to me. "Don't you worry. If Dad asks, I'll tell him I got it."

• • •

Dad didn't notice the mushroom garden until the third day.

Speech, occupational, and behavioral therapy. And now 'music therapy', too, Mom's newest addition that left my eardrums ringing. Chores to top it off, and a surprise virtual language class that Mom remembered only after the teacher sent a message. Our apartment was one part exhausted and two parts agitated from the activity-filled evening. Just as our collective engines were slowing, Dad burst through the door. Hot and excited.

"Austin, you ready? The Y closes in thirty minutes. We still got time to run some drills. Hurry up, get your basketball shorts on." Dad paused. A little bit of his light dimmed. He touched Mom's hand as she walked by. "You get my text?"

"My phone's in our room, charging. We just got done with Spanish. Check the calendar."

"You check the calendar," Dad said. "I put it in there. See? Drills. The Y. Six PM. Come on, Austin, let's go."

"They need to eat," Mom said.

"Then you should have fed them." Dad tried to reclaim his smile. "We'll get something on the way."

"Take Joey with you," Mom said. Before Dad could argue, she pounced. "Greg, don't you even. I been with these kids all day." Mom grabbed her shoes and wrapped her locs into a ponytail.

"Where you going?" Dad said.

"For a walk. You got this."

Mom left. Dad followed her out into the building hallway. They argued in that hushed way they did when in public.

Joey stood by the windowsill, staring at the mushroom garden. He needed transitions. Mom knew that. Dad knew that.

"We got to get ready for basketball, Joey," I said.

Joey stood very still. I looked over his shoulder. No way. Three little red bumps in the soil. They looked like the Advil pills Mom gave us for fevers, only smaller. Joey wet his little finger with the spray bottle, pulled up a flap of the plastic, and touched each of the bumps.

My heart swelled. Joey regularly latched onto many things, but none with as much devotion as this mushroom garden. And I had given it to him.

I was so full of pride that I didn't hear Dad come back in.

"What's this?" Dad held up the little brown box. Whereas just five minutes before, Dad had looked joyful and almost young, now he held the weight of the world. Scalp shining through thinning hair. Sweat-stained armpits. A line-etched face. Jaw set like a puppet's. Only not the kind that taught the ABCs or sang songs. The ones that looked dead and mean.

Joey stared with unblinking eyes as Dad inspected the box. My brother's head tilted with each turn of our father's wrist.

Dad knew. He remembered. I had to make it right.

"It's a m-m-m-mush, m-m-m-mush—"

"I can read, dammit." Dad knocked the flat of his palm against his own temple, just enough to slap! "I'm sorry. It's just, The Mushroom Garden? Didn't I put this back?" He turned to Joey. "Did you steal it?" A bit of hope traced Dad's question, as if Joey stealing meant he could turn out all right after all.

"He didn't s-s-steal it," I said. "I got it from the grocery store."

"So you paid for it?"

I said nothing.

"If you didn't pay for it, who did? Was Mom hiding in the other aisle? If not her, then who? I know I didn't."

"I thought it would b-b-b-be." I took a deep breath. Tears tickled my eyes. "I thought it would be a good toy for Joey."

"This isn't a toy," Dad said. He pushed the garden into Joey's waiting hands. My brother placed it back on the windowsill as if returning a fallen chick to its nest. Dad palmed the basketball. "This is a toy. Getting out there and playing with other kids, learning how to use your body, that's what you need. Stop that!" Joey had started to count the bumps. "Both of you, get ready." When neither of us immediately moved, Dad yelled.

"Now!"

• • •

We got to the Y fifteen minutes before closing, but Dad knew the manager. We had the court to ourselves. Dad's friend watched from the bleachers. Dad expected our gratitude. But I was hungry and cranky, and couldn't help asking, over and over again, why we had to play. And Joey . . . Joey was just being Joey.

"Tough luck," the manager friend said as we were leaving. "My youngest has some potential, but my oldest got two left feet and can't handle the ball to save his life."

"Thanks, Jay," Dad said.

We came home to the aroma of a quickly cooked meal. Dad crossed the apartment, grabbed the mushroom garden, and plopped it in the trash. Joey's scream curdled the air. Dad hesitated, retreated into his 'man-cave', and closed the door.

The mushroom garden peeked out of the top of the trash can. I took it out. I went up to Dad's door, knocked, and, when I heard permission, entered the closet-turned-sit-down space with a tablet mounted on the wall, pretending to be a television.

"Can he keep it?" I asked.

"What was that?"

I spoke louder. "Can he k-k-keep it?"

"That mushroom thing?" Dad ran his hand over what was left of his hair. "I don't get it. But you do. You understand him?"

"No," I said, because it was true. "But I like it that way."

Dad smiled. "You'll be a therapist one day, and then maybe you can help me. Come here, give me a hug."

This part I could understand. Dad smelled sweet and sour all at the same time.

"I'm sorry," Dad said. He was sorry a lot. Sometimes I didn't know what for. Other times, I knew but just didn't believe him. If he was sorry, why did he keep doing the things he was sorry for?

Joey peeked in. Dad brought him in for the hug, but Joey tried to pull away, as if our father was made of spiders instead of love. Dad frowned. Even I was annoyed. He's trying to love on us, Joey. Don't you see that?

Dad let us go. He patted me on the back and watched Joey with those tired eyes. My brother had forgotten all about the unwanted hug and was currently fascinated with how the door latch connected to the wall.

• • •

The mushroom garden continued to flourish. Soon it looked like a little field of spotted umbrellas. Joey watered them daily. Mom joked that Joey and I had inherited her green thumb. Dad injected some uncalendared sports activity whenever he saw us messing with the garden.

Joey began counting the caps, sometimes for hours at a time. Now, whenever Mom and Dad argued, Joey retreated to his windowsill and counted his mushrooms, as if one more would spontaneously pop up to save him. Or whenever Dad showed disappointment or frustration at the way Joey saw the world, Joey went to count his mushrooms. His count sped up at the end, willing there to be one more. But that's not how reality worked. A new mushroom wouldn't just spring up while he watched just because he wanted it to.

I hoped whatever fantasies my brother had, whatever salvations, that they included me. I thought they did.

• • •

Dad came in after work with excitement and a package. As he greeted Mom with a kiss, she held out her hand to take the new delivery.

But no. This was his. Dad opened the box and laid out a checkered cloth on the table.

"Come here, boys. I want to show you something."

"I have to pick up something from the store," Mom said. "I can take Joey with me."

"I want to show him, too," Dad said.

"You really think—"

"I do." Dad looked at Mom. "Let me try. Please."

Dad placed black and red plastic circles on the cloth. A trickle of sweat forming around his brow, he walked over to the kitchen counter where Joey was tending to his mushrooms.

"Joey," Dad said. "I'm going to teach you how to play checkers."

Joey started to count. Dad's nostrils flared, and his eyes blinked fast, like when he argued with Mom or when we'd just miss the train on the way to my school, the one that didn't take Joey because he wasn't 'normal enough', the one I was always late to because we had to drop off Joey first. Dad breathed in deep and mouthed a countdown from five. He'd just started the strange ritual a month ago. Was he becoming more like Joey? I didn't think so.

Joey brought his garden over to the table. I offered an explanation. "It-it-it makes him happy."

The checkers lesson started off well. I knew how to play from school, but pretended Dad was a good teacher. Then the focus turned to my little brother.

"The goal, Joey, is to take all my pieces," Dad said. "You take them like this."

Joey tried. Dad's redirects were gentle. When Joey made a move that didn't need correcting, Dad beamed.

"Yes! Just like that." Dad reset the pieces. Mom leaned against the doorway.

And then, things went downhill. Joey missed a trap. Dad triple jumped. Got to be more careful. Your turn, son. Joey counted mushrooms instead. Dad didn't understand. I did.

"Focus, Joey," Dad said. "It's your move."

Nerves grew around my brother. I knew because they reached out to me. Joey's count was off. He started again.

"Maybe that's enough for tonight?" Mom said.

"We're going to finish. He'll get it. He just needs time."

"It's late. And we have an early day tomorrow."

"I thought you were going to the store?" Dad said.

"I did. I got back half an hour ago. Dr. Jones said we shouldn't overstimulate him."

Dad leaned to grab the whiteboard calendar from the counter. "All this isn't overstimulating?"

"These are things he needs," Mom said.

"This is what he needs!"

Breathe, Dad, breathe, I thought.

But Dad didn't breathe. He stood and picked up Joey's mushroom garden. My brother lunged for it but only managed to cling to Dad's leg. Instead of chucking it into the garbage, Dad placed the garden far back on the table.

"Greg, can you please join me in the bedroom?" Mom said.

Dad folded up the checkers game and closed the box. "Fine," he said.

Joey stood on his tiptoes at the counter. He was about a foot out of reach.

"Maybe you shouldn't play with the garden so much, Joey," I said. Mom and Dad's door was closed. Loud music muffled any other sounds. "It's not a toy."

"Place the bag away from sunlight," Joey said, stretching. "Place the bag away from sunlight."

"Grow up," I said, and left him reaching for the garden.

• • •

Mom found new activities. One was called 'jasper' and another was for 'social skills'. Dad did more and more of his breathing exercises. In their own way, both fought to make Joey normal.

I wet the bed for the first time that year. Once, then twice, then I had to go back to wearing pull-ups. They itched; I woke scratching in the night.

Days passed. The apartment air thickened alongside the flourishing mushrooms. Dad tried again to connect. This time with a remote-controlled truck wrapped in a special casing.

"Greg," Mom said. The tiredness had her now, too. "What is this about?"

"He likes cars. It's the physicality of it. The sound. The texture. It's all in that book you gave me. I got this one specially made."

"How much did you spend?" Mom said. That car looked like it cost a lot of money. Maybe ten mushroom gardens' worth.

A shadow crossed Dad's face. "We spend thousands on class after class. We—"

"Okay, okay. I don't want to do this again, not in front of the kids. You got the receipt?"

Dad nodded. That rare joy was there, the kind he had for basketball. He stopped to talk to Joey. He even placed a gentle hand on the mushroom box: I come in peace.

"Daddy got you a real toy," he said. The car's metal and plastic shone bright and new. Joey looked from Dad to it, then down to his mushroom garden. He counted the caps that had grown through the slits. Ten. He counted them again. Still ten.

Dad slid the box out of his hand and replaced it with the remote control. Joey continued to count, his finger pointing to where each of the caps had just been. He always got ten.

Dad's smile leaned but didn't topple. He left for his man-cave, the mushroom garden still in his hand.

The toy car hadn't come with instructions. I had an idea. But had Dad bought it to 'fix' Joey? If so, would my idea help this sin? I shook my head of such thoughts and focused. I had no desire to 'fix' my brother. But things could be a little bit easier.

So I wrote out my own five golden rules for racecars on a piece of scrap paper. After finding an extra box in the small closet next to the front door, I packaged the new toy and presented it to Joey, trying to imitate the silent spark of finding the mushroom garden. But Joey continued to stare at the controller. The only sparks were for the mushrooms that weren't there.

Special, not different, I reminded myself.

"You're wondering where all the caps are, huh?"

Joey stopped and looked at me. The eyes that met mine held more than his five years. The hazel circles constricted and relaxed in a way I had never noticed before, almost a flutter, as if Joey was changing the focus on his perceptions, analyzing them in a whole new way. Joey knew more than I ever would. Part of that was knowledge of the cage we both lived in.

The connection was brief, and Joey's face returned to the blank stare that so exhausted Dad. He picked up the toy car, walked over to the windowsill, and positioned the automobile to perfectly catch the few minutes of evening sunlight. I realized I had been holding my breath and let out a long sigh. Then I went into the living room to watch television. Through tears that never fell, it all looked a blur.

• • •

Dad's rage woke me from TV-guided dreams.

This is it. This is the spanking. God, I hope it doesn't hurt.

But Dad's anger was far away and not for me. I sat up and listened past the television.

"What is this? Huh? What did you do?"

I jumped off the couch and ran to the bathroom. What I saw there didn't make sense. A dream . . . I must have still been in a dream. The tub was half-filled with brown water. The racecar, caked with slimy mud, floated in the middle. Joey stared at it as Dad held him at the shoulders and yelled in a way he only did with Mom before things got quiet for a while.

"Answer me! Why did you do this? Why do you hate me?"

I ran to my brother's side. I was afraid. Afraid Dad would spank, or Dad would leave. But mostly afraid for Joey. I could at least get close enough to remind Dad he had a son who could absorb his anger.

Mom came rushing out into the hall.

"Dee, I got this," Dad said.

"You obviously don't."

"You see the tub? Where do you think he got the dirt? Do you know how much this car cost us?"

"Cost you. What did you expect, Greg? That you could buy away your problems? What do you want from him?"

"What do you want from him?" Dad said. "Huh? If he's so okay, why are you trying so hard?"

And then, for the first time in his life, Joey answered a question. "If it doesn't grow," he said, "submerge it in water for twenty-four hours."

His father blinked. "What?"

"If it doesn't grow, submerge it in water for twenty-four hours."

Dad turned to me. "What's he saying?"

I couldn't explain. I only stood there, wide-eyed. Dad released his grip on Joey and fastened a lighter one on me. He rubbed my shoulders.

"You understand him, Austin. I know you do. What is it?"

"Greg . . ." Mom said.

"It-it-it . . ." I tried. I really tried.

"He knows." Dad shook me, just hard enough to make Mom start forward. Just enough to chase away my stutter. "Tell me. Please!"

"Greg!"

"It's from the instructions," I said. "F-f-for the mushroom garden."

Dad rubbed my shoulders again. "Show me. I want to see."

I ran. The instructions were buried under a pile of junk mail by the television. I paused at the sight of one of Mom's potted corner plants. It was a fern, as tall as me. The soil had been dug up like a grave.

Oh, Joey . . . Mom's on your side. Don't lose her, too.

Mom shifted to let me back in the bathroom, and Dad took the instructions and read them over. His face thinned. He read them again and handed them to Mom.

Mom read it twice, laughed, smiled, and put on her Joey-voice. "Honey, mushrooms don't grow out of cars. Nothing grows out of cars."

"Little girls play with gardens, and dolls, and ponies," Dad said. "Little boys like you play with toy cars. Do you understand?"

"That doesn't help, Greg."

"And you think what you're saying does?"

"If it doesn't grow," Joey said, "submerge it in water for twenty-four hours." He pointed to the tub, as if it explained everything.

"See!" Dad said.

Mom's smile wavered. She left the bathroom doorway and returned a second later with the mushroom garden. Joey's eyes lit up. Mom lowered to one knee and handed him the garden. "Water is for mushrooms and plants and people. Not cars. That's a . . . a . . ." Mom's voice broke, and my heart broke with it.

"Mom?" I said.

She turned to wipe away a lone tear. She never let us see her cry. Never. "That's a car. Here are your . . . your mushrooms."

"If it doesn't grow," Joey whispered, "submerge it in water for twenty-four hours." The words were slow, uneven. So sure before, now he sounded lost and confused, as if he could feel Mom and Dad's combined sorrow. Mom, who was always upbeat and hopeful. Mom, who fought her hardest to do best by us both. She now sounded defeated.

Dad massaged Mom's shoulders; she stood and leaned into him. He led her back to their room. Her sobs leaked out. They forgot to turn on the music.

"Am I doing it all wrong?" Mom said when her sobs began to quiet.

"There's no wrong." Dad's voice. "There's no right. You told me that. Hey. Hey . . . at least we know he can follow instructions."

Mom's sniffles cracked and formed into light giggles. Dad laughed, too. I looked at the tub. It wasn't funny. But it could be. Our parents' laughter was short-lived.

"There's a therapist I follow on social media," Mom said. "I'll reach out to her. Maybe it'll help."

"Yeah," Dad said. "Maybe."

I reached into the mud-tinted water and pulled the drain. Joey kept asking the floor if he should submerge it in water for twenty-four hours if it doesn't grow.

After several minutes, Joey ceased his questioning and left the bathroom. Mom's cries were full again. Dad's pacing footsteps vibrated the floor. Joey stared up at their locked door, down at his garden, then back to the door. He turned to sit against it, the mushroom garden in his lap. I sat beside him.

Joey counted the mushrooms over and over with a gaze that could cut glass. He counted faster, faster, as the sound of Mom's crying and Dad's pacing, both signs of wanting another life, another son, seeped out into the hallway. Ten. Ten. Ten.

"Onetwothreefourfivesixseveneightnineten, onetwothreefourfivesixseveneightnineten, onetwothreefourfivesixseveneightnineten, onetwothreefourfivesixseveneight . . . nine . . . ten . . ."

Joey stopped counting. I looked up. Joey pointed to a stub that hadn't been there before, poking up through the soil like a timid mouse, too curious about all the surface commotion to wait underground any longer.

"Eleven," Joey said.

The house was silent. Mom stopped her crying. Dad stopped his pacing. My five-year-old brother put the mushroom garden aside, scooted closer to me, and laid his head on my shoulder. "Joey, be good," he said.

I nodded. "Joey be real good."

# The Mushroom Garden, Neurodivergence, and Black Fatherhood

by Justin C. Key

My grandfather was a Washington, DC principal. He never acknowledged my father as his son. My dad, in turn, swore his children would know the sound of his voice. It was a low bar: I grew up knowing 'Dad' as only a footnote in my life. Now, as a devoted father of three, I'm breaking a small line of bad fathers. Too often, I feel I am sailing in uncharted waters, blind. I know where I don't want to go, and I haven't set my course based on simple, child-borne wants. I want the best for my kids. I question daily if I'm achieving it.

*The Mushroom Garden* is about the journey of raising a child with special needs. I am a husband. I am a father. I am a Black mental health professional. I am not a special needs parent. I have not experienced firsthand the dynamics of raising someone on the spectrum. The story instead pulls from my anxiety around raising Black boys and leans on my expertise as a psychiatrist, my intuition as a therapist, and my observations of society.

Raising any child is a complex endeavor. Drugs, sex, school performance, bullying, peer pressure, socializing—each crucial topic has its own cornucopia of theories and techniques. Of them all, I'd argue mental health can historically feel the most taboo, especially in Black and Brown communities. This stigma is a large reason I entered the field. My own grandfather died by suicide a year before I was born. No one talked about it. They told me he passed in his sleep until I stumbled across the truth as a teenager. Even now, some in my family maintain that just because he took his own life doesn't mean that he was 'mentally ill.'

In *The Mushroom Garden*, Greg is dealing with the internal and external pressures of getting this parenting thing right. He entered fatherhood remembering all he missed from his own absent father. He was probably overjoyed at the news that they were having a second boy. While his wife's bond grew daily with the tangible physical experience of growing their child, Greg bonded through fantasizing about Joey's future, about making up for what his childhood lacked. The things he would teach him—basketball, football, checkers—the talks they would have, even the challenges of adolescence around who was the 'man of the house'. It was all welcome. But Joey wouldn't fit into any of those dreams. Without a healthy realignment of Greg's expectations, every day felt like failure. Every misstep felt like a step closer to becoming what he was so desperately trying to avoid: like his own dad.

And then there's the strain on the marriage. Gender roles aside, two individuals coming together will inevitably have differing views on *some* aspect of child rearing. Often, they are benign, like whether the kids should shower and get into pajamas before or after dinner. Couples may talk about the big ones before children to make sure they make compatible parents, like religion, education, and even approaches to healthcare.

Neurodivergence, particularly in the Black community, can be blindsiding. Is autism even real or a bunch of propaganda? Shouldn't children conform to us, not the other way around? We've never been able to trust this nation's medical institutions; why would we defer to them *now*? Both parents strive for a happy kid but find themselves pulling in different directions. In the end, something has to give. The marriage. The hope. The bonds. Whatever the malady, the child suffers for it.

Greg needs to process. He needs to learn about himself, his insecurities, his assumptions, beliefs, and expectations. This is a lot; therapy can be quite difficult. As men, we're taught to suck it up and fix our own issues. Sitting with a therapist admits a need for help. It's an invasion of privacy. An unraveling of buried pains. A mirror that not only reflects what we see as ugly inside, but also the world that made us that way. But, for many, learning that one's child is on the spectrum brings forth resistance, anger, denial, and grief. Greg needs space, especially for this last: to mourn the kind of father he wanted to be, so he can grow into the father Joey needs.

Disclaimer time. As a writer of what I strive to be widely consumed fiction, I remain ever cognizant of what stereotypes I might propagate, even if they are true to my experience. Two things can be true: 1) my father was absent, and 2) the myth of the widespread absent Black father is grossly overblown. Throughout my life, I have seen and continue to see copious examples of beautiful Black fatherhood. As my generation ages, I see our Black fathers, on average, as present, devoted, active players in their children's lives. I credit at least some of this with the dismantling of mental health stigma, the ongoing conversation around masculinity, and, frankly, the deep want to build on the efforts of our parents' generation. 'They did the best with what they were given.' As we are slowly but surely being given the freedom to discuss our mental health, so will we.

# Life Size

by Reverie Koniecki

There were no locks on the bedroom doors of my childhood. Once, I made the mistake of trying to lock my mother out, but with one swift kick, she busted open the heavy wooden barrier. She was a third shift nurse at the hospital with perpetual bags under her eyes and achy feet as a result. She wore an A-line white uniform and a red-striped nursing cap that haloed her head. She nearly glowed with goodness, yet I found her pendulum terrifying. You couldn't know when she would detonate. She had two sets of moods during my childhood: entirely exhausted, tucked away in bed with darkening blinds choking the light, or an enraged tea kettle spewing obscenities.

I was seventeen the last time my mother put her hands on me. I got up that morning and put on my bathing suit and shorts. Most of my clothes were dirty, so I went into the hallway and dug one of her sweaters out of the Goodwill box. I came downstairs wearing it. Standing at the sink, she painted me with her gaze. The chill of the morning settled in the yellow kitchen. I shrank, staring at the cabinets that I'd helped her paint. There was a softness in the air. A calm that precedes the collision of opposing pressures.

*What are you doing wearing that?*

*--I am cold.*

*--That's trash, take it off. I spend good money on nice clothes for you, and you want to wear trash.*

*--No.*

The next thing I knew, she was on top of me, ripping the sweater off my body, thread by thread. She outweighed me, so escape wasn't an option. Yet I still tried to fight her off. By the time she was done, the sweater and my dignity were nothing more than shreds of yarn. I locked myself in my room. And by locked, I mean I stacked my furniture against the door so she wouldn't be able to kick it down. I didn't go to school or emerge for meals. My mother would come to the door periodically, but I assaulted her with my silence.

• • •

Two years after graduating from college, I moved to Boston and lived on my own for the very first time. I didn't realize that in the city, my salary was near the poverty level. When the bills came, I wasn't able to pay them. I turned to my familiar crying spells. I functioned at work, doing the minimum and barely keeping up. I couldn't concentrate. I felt as if the walls of my cubicle were shrinking. When I came home, I spent the evening paralyzed with terror. I was too embarrassed to ask for help. I started chain-smoking to ease some of the pressure. Smoking was better than crying. I don't know how many weeping sessions later, but I eventually got desperate enough to call a therapist. In my phone interview, I told the lady I was seeking help for budgeting. With a cigarette in my shaking hand, I sighed when I hung up. The days preceding my appointment stretched out like a yawn.

In our first session, the therapist took one look at my budget and said: "You don't need help budgeting. You need a second job." I sat there, mouth agape, processing her words. Depression clouded my thinking to the point where I couldn't see this obvious solution. All I could focus on was what I didn't have, instead of thinking my way out. I went to the mall the next afternoon and walked around filling out applications until I got a bite. When I went back to the therapist, my mood was much different. Elated even. I did not know that this was a part of the yo-yo mood cycle. I thought I could be happier if I could just change my circumstances, I would be alright. The therapist recommended we continue to see each other. I went to sessions with her until I took a pregnancy test. It came back positive. My pregnancy was the perfect explanation for my mood swings. I stopped going to therapy and slowly spiraled downwards until my next crisis.

• • •

The first time I went on antidepressants, I was pregnant with my second daughter. I couldn't stop crying. I spent my nights agonizing over how I was going to pay for daycare. I was so tired, I could barely work. I called in frequently because I couldn't get out of bed. My then partner spent most of his nights at the bars. Our relationship was the beginning of a long civil war. Once, I started to cry in the middle of my pelvic exam. Though I am sure many women have shed tears with their legs in stirrups and someone's hand in their vagina, it's still an awkward feeling. "Have you been feeling depressed?" My doctor asked. I nodded yes. My partner, who was in the room with us, remained silent as if he had been read his Miranda rights. The doctor told me to get dressed and to meet her in her office. Once there, she prescribed me an antidepressant and cautioned me that it wouldn't change my situation. I was confused. "He sat there and acted as if nothing was happening while you talked about your depression. There's no point in wasting your time with someone who doesn't want you. Believe me, been there, done that, and it leads nowhere," she said.

By the time I had my third child, my depressive episodes had grown closer and closer together until they overlapped. Sadness slowly became my normal. Chasing after three kids was more than exhausting, but doing it when you are depressed is like dragging your own dead body behind you. There is little joy. My children's childhood is marked by my discontent. My depression didn't allow me to enjoy them; I endured them. I'd lie on the couch with my face in the pillows while they ran circles around me. I would go up to smiling people and ask them how they did it. What magic did they have locked away? How can you smile as if there aren't grass fires everywhere? I'd ask. I live in the Bible Belt, so 90% of the time the answer was Jesus. But I'd tried Jesus and still felt like peeling my skin off.

I had this burning feeling to do something, but I couldn't focus it into anything tangible. I felt as though I was trapped and missing out on something. This made me sadder. I couldn't sleep. I felt as if I had a motor in me that wouldn't turn off, yet I was tired beyond belief. And the civil war between me and my partner raged on. We were broke. He was rarely there, and when he was, he ignored the fact that I was not okay. My suicidal ideations graduated into urges, and I checked myself into an intensive outpatient program. When I told my mother, she said: "You're not like those people." But I was. What we all shared in common was a romance with death. There was a spattering of people from all walks of life. One rich lady whose husband had run off with his secretary. A man who was living in a hotel with his pregnant fiancée and their two kids. A man who had witnessed his cousin's suicide at the age of thirteen and had been trapped in that memory ever since. A girl with red marks circling her neck. And then there was me, the woman who'd counted her pills and wondered how many it would take.

•••

After I was discharged, I went to a psychiatrist who diagnosed me with bipolar disorder. Still in denial, I took her prescription with the faith of a heretic. The drugs made me feel numb, so I stopped taking them. I didn't know what it felt like to be even. This would become my pattern over the next ten years. I would go to a psychiatrist, convince them that I didn't have bipolar disorder. And it worked. My following psychiatrists gave me a variety of diagnoses, including major depressive disorder, PTSD, generalized anxiety disorder, and attention deficit disorder. Anything was more suitable than bipolar disorder. When I did take the meds, they either made me too sleepy, made me gain too much weight, or didn't work at all. And if they did work, I'd go off of them once I felt better. The result was a serrated decade.

After I left my partner, I lost forty pounds within a month. My clothes draped around me like ceremonial robes. I couldn't sit still. I always felt like I had consumed 12 cups of coffee. I couldn't sleep. My boss asked me if I was sick. I told her that I had started taking vitamins and that had sparked me to eat healthier. My kids asked me why I didn't eat anymore. I redirected their attention. My body alternated between hot and cold. My hands and legs shook. I speed talked. I felt a mixture of euphoria and melancholy. I wrote without much coherence and unfocused vigor. I didn't know I was experiencing mania. I had become so good at explaining away my symptoms that I even convinced myself that nothing was wrong.

•••

My relationship with my mother was spotty at best during those pre-diagnosis years. She could be my biggest cheerleader one moment and, in the same breath, tear me down. And I was still angry over my childhood. I knew that she had done the best she could, given the tools at her disposal, yet I was at the mercy of her moods. When she would come home from those long nights at the hospital, I could tell by the jangle of her keys whether or not she was in a good mood. A hard gnashing of metal meant stomps up the stairs, screams about some indiscretion, maybe an ass-whooping, and definitely the swinging open of bedroom doors. When the notes tinkled softly, so was her disposition.

•••

"You scare me in the mornings," my daughter once told me. Our mornings usually began with me barging into the kids' rooms and climaxed with me screaming at them to hurry up. I once hollered at my son on the morning of his standardized state test, and he failed it. I turned our mornings into moments of terror. It was an all too familiar scene, except it was my ticking bomb.

After my divorce, I moved across town. My daughter, who was of driving age, shuttled her siblings back and forth between her father's house, school, and my house. I had just had surgery on my foot and spent most of the day zonked out on painkillers. I was still unmedicated and was on the crying spell cycle again. I didn't know that the painkillers caused my mood to do acrobatics. On this particular day, I woke up early and checked her room. She wasn't there. The tectonic plates in my head crashed into one another, causing chunks of my composure to break off and cloud my sea of vision. My manias are life-size. I don't even realize I am in one until long after the damage is done. I called her father and got no answer. I called my daughter and got no answer. I spent the next fifteen minutes alternating between dialing their phone numbers until finally my ex picked up. I had had time to work myself up, so my ideas were scattered. My daughter joined the conversation, and I screamed at her about not calling or texting. I called her a bitch, which of course set her off. "You're the bitch," she yelled back. The screaming continued until she came home. When she walked through the door, she threw the keys onto the floor. We argued off and on over the hours, caught in a dance that neither of us knew how to end. At one point, she mocked me. Something snapped like a twig underfoot. The next thing I knew, I forgot about the stitches in my foot and pounced on her. My husband and my other daughter pulled us apart while my son pleaded for me to stop.

• • •

"How do others respond to you?" my current psychiatrist asked on my first visit. He explained that oftentimes it's the ones closest to you that show you that something is wrong. I recoiled and gave my best professional, it's okay smile. He didn't smile back. He asked me why I stopped taking my meds in the past. I explained to him that they didn't work. He told me I wasn't taking the right meds. "You have bipolar disorder," he said with deadpan eyes. I tried the dance I did with previous doctors. I didn't want to believe it. *But...* I started. "You were able to convince others that you don't have this disease, but you do."

When my mother stopped working third shift, she became a different person. The dark circles and stony look on her face disappeared. She became more patient, and her explosive anger cooled. As a grandmother, she was by far more patient than she was as a mother. She and I get along now, mostly because I stopped trying to punish her for the past. There came a point when I understood, and that was enough.

I am now well medicated and haven't had an episode in years, though I sometimes resent how much I need to take to be well. Two pills in the morning, three at night, and a monthly injection. My psychiatrist sees me as his success story. I'm consistent and even. I haven't had a crying spell in ages, and my relationships are healthier. Now my check-ins consist of fifteen-minute phone calls every six months.

I recently finished teaching a unit on Oedipus Rex, and my students are struck by the irony behind Oedipus' declaration to hunt down and punish King Laius' murderer when, unbeknownst to him, he is the monster. When it is revealed that Oedipus is not only the murderer of his father, but has married his mother, my students are appalled and disgusted. "Isn't that illegal?" One girl blurted out, "Is he f—ing his mom?"

I explain to them that Oedipus' journey symbolizes our own quests to reveal our true identities. "We are blind to ourselves," I say. They are not impressed. I try to explain to them that it takes a collision to see the truth. But they see no likeness.

# Door into the Mind of My Mother

by André Le Mont Wilson

"Andre, I found something."

Over the phone, my brother, Terry, choked with tears. Did he find *Woman in Pain*—the wood carving our father gave our mother when they first met? I pressed the receiver to my ear. "Is it Fred's sculpture?"

Terry sobbed. He dribbled words one at a time, "No . . . it's . . . Mom's . . . writings."

"What's it about?"

"I can't tell you over the phone."

*What couldn't he tell me over the phone? Why the tears?*

I changed my strategy to snatch the information from him. "Could you scan and email it?"

"No, I'll just wait until you get here."

Terry piqued my interest. I had planned to travel to Los Angeles the next day to attend the memorial jewelry show that my father's widow, Kristen, staged at the home of his former pottery student. I cracked my knuckles. My hands ached to grip the manuscript Terry found. *A clue to our parents' marriage?*

• • •

I flew to LA and stepped into my mother's apartment. It's strange how I referred to it as "my mother's apartment" as if she still lived here. My siblings, Terry and Joi, had drawn the blinds. Shadows pervaded the rooms. A mountain of brown flowers, once yellow, including those that had lain on our mother's casket, decayed on the dining room table. The memorial service had occurred three months earlier.

As I sat on my mother's bedroom floor, I sorted her boxes of papers on the spot where she had died—a green patch of carpet beaten down from foot traffic and from her praying on her knees. I heard breathing and footsteps behind me. I turned. My brother Terry teetered in the doorway, papers in his trembling hands, tears in his eyes. "This is what I found."

I grabbed the sheets. The typed pages appeared brittle. The room darkened as I read.

• • •

**After the Sun Went Down**

*The door slammed behind my husband as he left for court. Little did it appear, that January morning, that the year 1959 was always to stand out in my memory as an awakening. Since the night had a definite effect on me, my life was to reach an all-time low in a struggle for sanity. Alone we stood, my two sons, and me—pregnant.*

*We lived in Aliso Village, one of the many housing projects in Los Angeles. Alcoholics, dope addicts, prostitutes, and people who used Aliso as a steppingstone to a goal in life here, too. I was not a part of their worlds; my world was painfully different—the world of the mentally ill.*

• • •

*"Struggle for sanity." "The world of the mentally ill."* I reread those phrases before I proceeded to read what happened next when her first husband—a philandering Korean War vet—walked out on her, two kids, and a baby on the way.

• • •

*The boys and I were now receiving Public Assistance; there wasn't a financial worry. Still, twice a week, I visited the out-patient psychiatric clinic, trying to free myself of this alien personality which was my constant companion.*

...

*With all my efforts, there was still no way of keeping my two-year-old from knowing the agony my mind and body were going through. Although the door to my bedroom was closed and my head covered, he would come in and ask, "Mommy, why are you crying? Who hurt you?"*

*Feeling ashamed that he had caught me again, "Nothing," I would say. "Nothing. Just go back to your room." Time after time, this would happen while I was quietly sniffling, trying to get out a cry after the boys went to bed. It amazed me that he always knew.*

*Finally, . . . whenever I sensed an attack of depression coming, I would go in the bathroom and lock the door. While the water was running in the bathtub, I could cry unheard. My body trembled, I felt caged, and I desired to be free of these bounds. There was no trust in myself around the children during an attack. I might become violent and hurt them, for deep in my being was a strange aversion to small children.*

*Alone in the living room, I would go from wall to wall—sometimes even hitting them. Just to have been able to cling to the walls and walk on the ceiling would have been a relief. When deeply depressed, I would scratch myself and grip my hands. There was a desire to cut my wrist and get out of this living hell.*

• • •

*One of my attacks landed me in the county hospital with a miscarriage. This was to be my longest night. After an examination and many questions, a specific room was assigned to me. I felt suspended between two worlds, but I could hear the doctor telling the nurse, "She'll probably need an operation later on."*

*At the word "operation," my life started backward. Suddenly, I wasn't in the hospital anymore. Instead, there lay a little girl who had been hit by a baseball in the pelvic region many years ago. The doctor represented a doctor my mother had taken me to, and the nurse was my mother. I remembered the doctor whispering in the other room as if it were now, "She may never have children, and even if she does, there will probably be an operation later on."*

*Never once in all these years had I thought of the doctor's prediction. However, in my subconscious mind, it was bothering me. I realized that was the clue to what I had tried to tell the psychiatrist many times. All I knew to say was, "It's just something about babies that bothers me." At night, I would try to draw my fears, but to no avail. My drawings never progressed beyond a certain point—a woman wanting to go out the door, and in big letters I would write the word "BABIES" in front of her.*

*Somehow, my childish mind had conceived the idea that having a baby was the worst thing that could happen to a woman. It was quite plain to me why I had been resentful toward the children at times. I really believed childbirth could contribute to the operation the doctor had predicted.*

*As the night wore on, I was given more sleeping pills, but sleep continued to evade me. My mind was running away with ideas. I wanted to talk to somebody. Finally, I asked for a doctor, but he could not help me. Only one person could help—my psychiatrist.*

*. . .*

*As I stepped off the ward elevator, at the desk sat the psychiatrist busily studying my chart. . . I tried to tell him about my strange reliving of an ugly childhood experience. He was wise and suggested I wait and talk at the clinic. My appointment was the next day. I knew, and he knew, as I tried to tell him, this experience was the door I had tried to open in vain for many months.*

*I welcomed leaving the hospital because I could accept my children more fully. Even though I knew my marriage was over, the thought of facing life with two sons wasn't frightening. A different Mommy would be coming home to four little waiting arms.*

• • •

I finished reading with tears in my eyes. Now I knew why Terry would not share her essay over the phone or email. I turned to him in the doorway, "Mom had a miscarriage and mental illness?"

He nodded. "Yes."

My earth quaked. A tsunami of grief engulfed me. Each wave pulled me further into the ocean. First, I grieved over the loss of a brother or sister I never knew. Second, I grieved over my mother's statement "that having a baby was the worst thing that could happen to a woman." *I was her nextborn. Did she want me? Did my birth stop her from going out the door and achieving her dreams?* I felt survivor's guilt for being born. Third, I grieved over the depression she experienced. If she had succeeded in her "desire to cut (her) wrist and get out of this living hell," I would not have been born four years later.

Questions swirled around my mother. *Was mental illness a factor in her first husband, Mickie Thompson, abandoning her? Forgetting the wedding vow of "in sickness and in health," couples experience a high rate of divorce if one of them struggles with mental health issues. Since she had a mental breakdown in 1959 following her first divorce, what happened a decade later following her second?* I don't have any answers.

Another question I cannot answer is, "Was she mentally ill when she raised me?" I searched my past for clues to my mother's mental state. Nothing screamed "crazy" to me. Perhaps I was so close to her and lived so long with her that everything seemed "normal." I thought I knew my mother because she raised me, but I soon realized that I didn't know her well enough. I felt helpless, like when my brother Terry, aged two, stood in our mother's doorway and asked, "Mommy, why are you crying? Who hurt you?"

The back of my index finger wiped tears from my eyes. I ceased trembling, straightened my back, and handed the essay back to my brother. "Make a copy for me."

I scanned the cluttered room. Unread papers filled unsorted boxes. I resumed my tone as the lead investigator. "This is why we have to sort through Mom's stuff carefully. We don't know what else she has hidden."

"I know."

• • •

After I returned home, I called my brother with a follow-up question. "Terry, do you remember the story you found about Mom being committed to a mental hospital?"

"Yes."

"Do you recall a period in your childhood when Mom didn't live with you?"

I heard silence on the other end of the phone. Terry broke it, "Come to think of it . . . there was a period when Mom did not live with us." *Us* being him and our oldest brother Dion

"How long was it?

"Oh, a couple of weeks . . . maybe a month."

*Mom was in a mental hospital for a month. Her essay made it sound like she stayed a couple of days.*

"What happened to you guys? Who took care of you?"

"We went to live with Aunt Edna up in Oakland, and then she came down to live with us in Los Angeles. Grandma Dawson came to live with us, too, and Cousin Thaddeus. We were living on 57th Street then."

I opened the kitchen drawer, grabbed a marker, and wrote notes on the dry-erase board fixed to the refrigerator. "When was this?"

"About 1961."

*1961? That was two years after the events chronicled in our mother's essay, but two years before her marriage to Fred. Are we talking about the same committal to the psychiatric ward, or did she have a relapse after her essay concluded with "a different Mommy would be coming home to four little waiting arms"?*

"Did anyone explain anything to you about what was happening to Mom?"

"No one explained anything to me."

"Did you notice any difference when Mom came back from the hospital?"

"I really couldn't tell any difference. She was her regular Mom self."

# Blank

by Chris TPG Green

We watched the sweet words of our grandmothers transmute to bitter wine,
*The mind, a terrible thing to break.*
Age the wrecking ball.
Watch her daughter's play Jenga, pull out the false identity formed daily
Hoping to keep as much safe before the tower falls.

We watched our grandfathers' will bend and body break,
Lose strength they were forced to pass down,
Become more vulnerable than ever allowed to be,
Watched us sons carry them when the sun set
The mind shrouded in darkness.

Dementia, demonizes a family
The way it puts them through hell.
Wish for Heaven to send death for our loved ones.

Back then...they never knew how to define such a turn of mind,
Such a bend of soul and spirit.
Elderly blacks cast back into the night
Dying amongst strangers in facilities.

What facilitates a body to bury itself under disease?

To edit a human being.

If it ever comes for me, I hope my body will auto-correct.
I'm looking at my mother and father
hoping they aren't close to turning the page,
or going
blank.

# Chatter

by Chris TPG Green

When he talks to me
His eyes dart around the room like they're seeing angels.

When he talks to his wife
His tongue motions like he communes with Devils,

Slick and foul.

She don't know what kinda hell he'll raise,
Or what the demons in his head say,
Or if he hears the angels in his ear pray,

Or if he's only prey.

Can't tell cause he always plays victim.
Everyone out to get him.

Literally,

The kids call him crazy,
Skips medication daily,
Complains it makes him hazy.
Combination of things that conclude he's never clear
Walking mental fog, but he sees paradise on the other side of inner voices.
A slice of silence only sleep provides,
A constant tug of war for mind control
He never has a tight grip.

He's slipping. More into the chatter
He's lost
More than in his head.

The separation moves to the heart...

But I ask myself...
Is it his fault?

Where does he fade
and schizophrenia have its way?

# Auntie Impossible

by Nicole J. Evans

watched her wither where she chose to stand still
watched her 'til eyes turned to dust
there's no such thing as disbelief
once witnessed

when we were little, she said to
make sure we kept watch as she
walked next door lest the boogeyman
or boo-boo the fool be out there

made sure not to avert our eyes
and count the times she locked the door
so when she asked if she did
we could assure her

said a fungus exists that makes your hair fall
out in patches / turns smooth skin
the texture of orange peel / causes low self-esteem
heart attacks / unwed pregnancies
leaves eggs of glitter flecks on your skin

won't eat food unless the dates have been checked
or she's sure it wasn't the first item on the shelf,
please make sure you pull from behind / please, leave
her groceries on the porch to the left on top of the makeshift
protective mat made out of garbage bags / please, ensure
each item is bagged separately and make sure you update
her as you leave each store / leave the house / when you arrive

she'll ask for a minute but take maybe five
she's trying to make sure she stays alive
a neighbor is crossing the driveway with no mask on

she only needs you to retrieve her medicines
like the Clonazepam carelessly prescribed that marries
addiction with whatever mental illness she refuses
to get diagnosed/ her original formula classic vanilla Ensure
her mac-n-cheese-mashed-potatoes sans gravy
from a very specific KFC / her Sprite / her Farmer John
Beef Franks NOT wieners – there's a difference

and she's trying to keep her weight up
lest she dwindle down to nothing

her 1-minute quick oatmeal / her hazelnut Carnation creamer
a 40-pack of Crystal Geyser bottled water and
Glad trash bags / she no longer wants C&W frozen spinach
which you can only get at Smart and Final so you have no
idea how she gets her nutrients outside of her Centrum 50+
Women's gummies / heavy-duty 10-inch paper plates
that she assures work amazingly as both a fan and a platter

we help her but can't recall the last request for soap at all
or a time when she didn't screen every phone call
or would answer the door or let anyone in
no matter what was happening

she has always questioned everyone's capability
dresses in black that tatters and fades, but we pretend
it is as new as she needs it to be
we pick blind instead of reality

we take turns until turns took us
to ventures she couldn't fathom
questions we couldn't bear to know the answers to,
not that she would spill the truth

we held behind tight lips until we tittered about
the glitter egg-flecked fungus and rust-hued roaches
in containers since babies, we knew this was casual
always wonder why she chose to stay close to the womb
perhaps she knew the mind she could lose
holding distance didn't prevent that

so common and private
bound in isolation
forgive me, she doesn't deserve
to die the way she chooses
she deserves more

# Family Dynamics: Discussion Questions

Use these questions to spark conversation about the poems, stories, and essays in this section.

## The Mushroom Garden

by Justin C. Key

1. Is the relationship the mother has with her sons better or simply different than the relationship the father has with them?

2. Would you describe Greg and Dee as being happily married? What are some of the stressors in their relationship? What strategies are they using to work towards a healthy relationship? In the long run, do you think they will be able to navigate their commitment to parenting and their love for one another?

3. From the beginning of the story, we can see how the narrator has internalized his father's opinions. He hears the difference in the way his Mom and Dad refer to Joey and lets the reader know how he feels. Do you think his Mom or Dad notices his feelings?

4. The narrator is willing to spend time playing a game he dislikes. Why? How do you think this will impact the narrator later on? What type of relationship can you foresee between the narrator and his Dad, and the narrator and his Mom?

5. What do the mushrooms symbolize?

6. While there are books on parenting, learning to parent is on-the-job training. We don't get to erase attitudes, comments, and disappointments. Each day is a new opportunity for parents and children to learn and grow together. In this family, as in all relationships, there is a search for reconciliation between expectations and acceptance. We can see and hear the father's disappointments and frustrations, but we can also see and hear the narrator's hopes and uneasy feelings. What advice would you give the different family members, or what do you hope for each one of them?

7. How does the essay, "The Mushroom Garden, Neurodivergence, and Black Fatherhood," impact your experience of reading the story? Does it make a difference to you that it is creative nonfiction?

---

## Life Size
by Reverie Koniecki

1. At first glance, it seems as though the author has the same behavior patterns as her mother, which would lead the reader to suspect the mother also has bipolar disorder. Do you think the mother had bipolar disorder, or are there other reasons for the mother's behavior?

2. *I live in the Bible Belt, so 90% of the time the answer was Jesus. But I'd tried Jesus and still felt like peeling my skin off.* Do you think the stigma of seeking mental health help is greater in the bible belt than in other parts of the country?

3. The author's mother tells her, "You're not like those people." Why do you think she says this? What if the daughter listened to the mother, because she is a nurse? What does her mother's response say about stigma?

4. The author admits that she does not like the amount of medicine she needs to take to maintain a level of mental wellness. Do you have an opinion on taking medication? Do you make a distinction between taking medication for physical or mental health?

5. The narrator makes a comparison between the classic Greek play, Oedipus, when she says, "We are blind to ourselves." Her students fail to see the connection. If you are familiar with the play, can you relate to the narrator's statement? Have you seen generational patterns of repetition in your life?

---

## Door Into the Mind of My Mother
by Andre Le Mont Wilson

1. Even though the narrator's mother is deceased, his mother's experience with mental illness impacts him. He grieves the miscarriage; he has survivor's guilt and is empathetic to the way his mother said she felt about not having another child. He also grieves the emotional symptoms of suicidal ideation that his mother endured. Do you think the mother wanted her sons to know about this time in her life? This new information strengthens the narrator's resolve to continue searching through his mother's things. Do you think this is healthy, or just part of the overall grieving process?

2. According to a 2024 study, the National Alliance of Mental Illness (NAMI informs us that one in five adults experiences mental illness each year, and one in twenty experiences serious mental illness each year. In the essay, the author tells us

that *couples experience a high rate of divorce if one of them struggles with mental health issues*. He then feels his father abandoned his mother, and the vow of "in sickness, and in health" was not honored. What do you think about the percentage of divorces in this country, the information from NAMI, and the author's questions about his parents' divorce?

3. Many parents discuss their physical health history with their adult children. Do you think parents should discuss their mental health history with their children?

---

## Blank and Chatter
by Chris the Poetic Genius Green

1. How do the different diagnoses of the people in Blank and Chatter impact the perspectives and experiences of the poet and the family?

---

## Aunty Impossible
by Nicole J. Evans

1. In this poem, the speaker says the aunt in the story deserves more. What do you think she deserves, and how can she be better served?

2. Do you think the aunt needs mental health services?

# Faith and Mental Health

*Mental Health in Black families is often ignored*
*and placed in a box for God to take care of,*
*but we know that mental illness is a real issue*
*that needs space and room to be addressed and treated.*
*Having a mental illness is not a character flaw.*

—Mental Health America

# Exploring Black Mental Health Through a Christian Lens

by Pastor Samuel J. Casey

In the Black community, conversations around mental health often carry both **sacred weight and social stigma**. Yet when we look through a Christian lens, we find that faith offers not only a source of strength but also a divine framework for healing and restoration. Scripture reveals that even the greatest of God's servants, such as Elijah, David, and Jesus Himself, wrestled with emotional fatigue, inner conflict, and profound anguish. Their stories remind us that faith and mental struggle are not opposites; they are often companions on the same spiritual journey.

**Elijah in the Cave: When Success Feels Heavy**

In 1 Kings 19:9–18, we find Elijah in a cave — weary, afraid, and isolated. He had just experienced one of his greatest triumphs, calling down fire from heaven and proving that Yahweh is God. Yet afterward, he sank into despair, saying, "It is enough; now, O Lord, take away my life."

Elijah's story reveals that even moments of great victory can be followed by profound weariness. Success does not shield us from fatigue, self-doubt, or fear. Many of us know that feeling — the quiet pressure to sustain momentum, to appear strong, or to carry the weight of expectations. Elijah's encounter prompts us to examine the **mental maps and internal narratives that shape our understanding** of God's presence in times of distress.

In verses 11–12, God tells Elijah to stand on the mountain and watch as He passes by: "And behold, the Lord passed by, and a great and strong wind tore the mountains and broke in pieces the rocks before the Lord, but the Lord was not in the wind. And after the wind and an earthquake, but the Lord was not in the earthquake. And after the earthquake, a fire broke out, but the Lord was not in the fire. And after the fire, the sound of a low whisper."

Elijah was accustomed to God showing up in power, fire, wind, and thunder, but this time, God came in a whisper. That "still small voice" required Elijah to shift his expectations and quiet his spirit. The assignment on his life didn't change, but his heart was renewed to fulfill it. Sometimes God heals not by changing our circumstances but by changing how we listen.

**David: Practicing Soul Care Through Worship**

Before David ever wore a crown, he learned to care for his soul. On the hillsides of Bethlehem, tending his father's sheep, he cultivated resilience through music, worship, and prayer. When the lion and the bear attacked, David learned courage in solitude — lessons that prepared him for Goliath in public. In today's terms, David modeled what we might call "spiritual self-care." Through the Psalms, he processed grief, anxiety, fear, and hope, turning emotional pain into prayerful poetry. In Psalm 42:11, David writes:

"Why, my soul, are you downcast? Why so disturbed within me? Put your hope in God, for I will yet praise Him, my Savior and my God."

David reminds us that naming our pain before God is not a lack of faith; it is an act of trust. His **worship was both therapy and theology**, a rhythm of honesty and hope that allowed him to face life's giants without losing his peace.

### Jesus in Gethsemane: The Model of Holy Vulnerability

Perhaps the most profound example of emotional honesty and mental anguish comes from Jesus in the Garden of Gethsemane (Matthew 26:36-46; Luke 22:39–46). On the eve of His crucifixion, Jesus withdrew with His closest disciples to pray. The Gospels tell us He became deeply distressed and troubled, and He confessed, "My soul is overwhelmed with sorrow to the point of death."

In this sacred moment, Jesus — the Son of God — reveals the depth of His humanity. He does not suppress His anguish or perform strength for others. Instead, He kneels and pours His heart out to the Father: *Father, if it be possible, let this cup pass from me. Nevertheless, not my will, but Yours be done.* This is not weakness; it is holy vulnerability. Jesus teaches us that true faith is not the denial of struggle but the courage to bring our struggle before God. His sweat, "like drops of blood," reveals the physical toll of spiritual pressure, reminding us that our emotional battles are real and worthy of compassion. And yet, in the midst of agony, the text tells us that an angel appeared and strengthened Him. The help of heaven came through His honesty, not in spite of it.

For the Black community, a people who have endured generations of trauma and triumph, Gethsemane is a sacred mirror. It shows that lament and faith can coexist. It affirms that vulnerability is not weakness, and **seeking help, both spiritually and professionally, is an act of courage**. Jesus' example permits us to be fully human and wholly faithful at the same time.

### Faith, Therapy, and the Path Toward Wholeness

For generations, the Black Church has been the sanctuary where faith and resilience meet. Prayer, worship, and the Word have sustained us through slavery, segregation, and social struggle. But faith also calls us to wisdom and wholeness — to pray earnestly and to seek wise counsel when needed.

There is no shame in therapy, and no contradiction in seeking a counselor while trusting in God. In fact, professional help can be one way God answers our prayers. As James 1:5 reminds us, "If any of you lacks wisdom, let him ask of God, who gives generously." We must continue to teach that prayer and professional support are not opposing forces — they are complementary pathways to healing.

So, take it to the Lord in prayer. Rise from your knees and walk out what you've prayed for. And if the burden feels too heavy, seek the help God provides through those trained to guide us toward peace. Because the same God who met Elijah in a whisper, who strengthened David in worship, and who sent angels to comfort Jesus in the garden — still meets us today.

# Neurodivergent

by Jay Writes

It's time,
time that my concept of it would stop eluding me.
Haven't eaten nor drank,
Thirst unquenched as a political prisoner.
A hellish heavenly debate ensues,
Consuming me whole in a monster fashion.

Why did God make me neurodivergent?

The conversation ends, but the one within continues
*Saying, I'm doing just fine.*
Then suddenly, internal gears grind with grit,
screeching to a halt.

My mind is a beautiful catastrophe.

You may not believe, nor understand,
my mind fly fishes, fluently,
swimming through thoughts
at the speed of sound and light,
*I sleep both sound and light.*
Sleep deprivation: a familiar phone, and my solemn friend.
The neurodivergent mind loves rewards.
There's always a voice whispering,
*Take debate, take de - bait.*

Horns and halo struggle on each of my shoulders.
They battle to the death
Yet no victor emerges. I am the only casualty.

I realize after death
no one will know our thoughts, just our actions.
Yet the ADHD mind is crippled by thoughts
to the point of inaction.

Here I stand broke but unbroken.
Breaking chains, yet yearning possession,
enslaved to the flesh of my own body.
Embodied, it's a blessing to wake up every day
This beautiful catastrophe feels it's time.
If I can love others, I can love my own mind.

# Resurrection

by Alexander James

Depression turns bedrooms into cemeteries,
turns headboards into tombstones.
Blankets become thick soil to bury yourself underneath.

Getting out of bed requires an excavation,
an archeological dig to find
a reason to try again.

When you are held by sadness's grip,
every bed is a waterbed.
And somehow you are drowning in yourself.

Church folks say just get over it.
You are husband.
You are father.
You are believer.
You are a leader.
But I have learned how quickly titles
can become a tidal wave.
Instead of life rafts,
titles become your life.
And titles are no life at all.

The chip on your
shoulder will become
the stone they roll in front of your tomb.

But the voice of good friends
becomes the lungs of Christ
calling us out of our own graves.

I have been resurrected by
text messages from thoughtful friends.

You would be amazed how holy
*Thinking* about you can be to
a dry soul.

# Thirst

by Lydia Theon Ware i

Well water,
Drinking tainted water,
swallows the effort to be filled with joy.
Bucket rusty, rope frayed,
afternoon rain spills into the well,
hoping to hide from the sun.

He was thirsty, and yet he sat without drinking.
He was tired; he had not yet eaten,
and his friends were not with him.

Sometimes he felt like the sun was punishing his need.
Sometimes he felt like the water was dry.
Sometimes he felt like his mind would crumble
like swollen dust beneath lost fingertips.
He wanted to laugh, but it would not come.

At last, a woman approached slowly.
Her heart sank; she would not be able to cry today.
They stared at each other.

The empty bucket heard their hesitation.
Sometimes, it's all you can do to not run away from connection.
They spoke briefly. The rain increased.
The well began to overflow.
His sorrow lifted, if only for a moment.

# The Stigmatism

by Anjetta (Anjie) Williams-Brown

The Black and Brown skins are resilient
They made it through slavery
They made it through segregation

Depression is for the Caucasian

We are blessed we have no reason to be depressed
Black and Brown stand strong in the Spirit

We don't get depressed
Only the weak in spirit are depressed
Black and Brown don't get depressed

When will the stigmatism end

Black and Brown do get depressed
Black and Brown are afraid to talk about it
Black and brown will be branded

Black and Brown do get depressed
When can there be help
Without being branded with the scarlet "D"

The Black and Brown need help

# Chaos

by Marcus Thompson

I'm not suicidal but the ever-increasing thoughts that I do not want to be here echo in my mind with malicious intent. The weight is almost unbearable, this relentless pulling and stretching of my mind has begun to plant seeds that bear no fruit.

The sense once made overshadowed by chaos, choked by thorn vines, brittle from drought birth now given to despair to this single underlying feeling of hopelessness. I feel hopeless.

My point escapes me, like the juvenile idea that there was purpose to any of this to begin with. I speak to God almost daily, and *I'd be lying if I said the image of a man holding conversation with himself doesn't creep in from time to time.* If ever a time for clarity, it's now Lord! I need answers,

Trying to make sense of these thoughts in my head is like a playlist of the alphabet on shuffle. I know what it should be, I just can't put it together, and I know anyone listening would tell me to hold on for better.

I just don't see it.

# What the Preacher Said

by Anjetta (Anjie) Williams-Brown

*Depression is an evil spirit.*
*If you have depression you are possessed by the devil.*
*God don't make you depressed, Satan does,* he said.

How can I be possessed?
I'm God's child.
I'm not possessed.

*Black and Brown people don't get depressed,* he said.

Depression knows no color.

My head is foggy.
I can't think;
I know there is a cure.

If I say I'm depressed

No one will talk to me,

Cause the preacher said

*Depressed people are possessed.*

*I can't tell Mama,*

She'll think I'm possessed.

*Can't tell grandma,*

She'll think I'm possessed.

Who will help me?

I'm not possessed.

Maybe it's the preacher that's possessed!

I need a little help

Cause I'm not possessed.

I'm God's child.

# My Daily Meds.

Model and Photographer: Alora Young

# Reclaiming My "No"

by Dr. Ahliah Sharp

Daughter, Sister, Wife, Mom, Momma's baby, Daddy's girl.
I've held many titles,
but titles that are hardest to shake
are the ones that created my destiny.

The title *Survivor.*
*Survivor* suggests I faced death and made it,
means someone in my situation didn't make it.
To survive an act of terror or trauma and still rise,
I *Survive*!

My previous title was *Victim.*
I didn't ask to be beaten.
I didn't ask to have my ***No*** taken from me.
For him, ***No*** seemed like a suggestion
that quickly became an option,
that could easily be ignored.
left me believing that ***No***, is not a word
I am allowed to use
because it came at a cost
I could no longer afford to pay.
It became easier to just say yes,
because at least then, I had no scars, no wounds.
I could pretend I had the choice,
and it was actually an option.
Don't judge me!
I believed that giving in
would make me stronger in the end.
It made me disappear.

But God saw me.
All roads lead to God,
scripture, church, gospel music,
earning my master's in psychology.
Practicing individual, and group therapy,
with every client I had
I realized I was ultimately counseling me.

Then, one day, I- chose – me!
I took my first breath,

as if I literally escaped the vaginal canal,
departing my mother's womb,
Reborn.
Victim no more!

# What I Discovered

by Tona Farlow

My name is Tona Farlow, and I am a Licensed Marriage and Family Therapist — but that was not always my story. I grew up in Bay Shore, Long Island, New York, in a blended family of nine children — seven girls and two boys. As the baby of the bunch, I got a front-row seat to life happening from every angle. I watched joy, struggle, resilience, and dysfunction all play out in real time.

At fifteen, I became a teenage mother. People told me I would never amount to anything, my choices had written my life story — and not in my favor. For a while, I wondered if my pregnancy embarrassed my parents more than it disappointed them. The treatment I received from some healthcare professionals only deepened that wound; they seemed determined to make me pay for my *mistake*. Their judgment was cruel, but it didn't break me. Instead, it fueled me.

I took responsibility for my choices, kept my head in the books, and worked part-time weekends at Burger King. I graduated high school summa cum laude — on time — while raising a baby. I also spent a year and a half in a voluntary program for teenage mothers. The goal was simple: work or go to school. I did both.

After graduation, I received a full scholarship to the State University of New York at Farmingdale to study nursing. I knew I wanted to help people, but nursing wasn't what I imagined. *Something in me knew* there was a more fulfilling path for me to take. After my parents divorced, I moved with my mother to Santa Barbara, California, and attended Santa Barbara City College, majoring in Liberal Studies. That's where I discovered my fascination with criminal justice. I wanted to understand what motivated people — what led them down certain paths.

I went on to earn a bachelor's degree in criminal justice from the University of Central Texas, graduating with honors. Soon after, I began my career in law enforcement, working in probation. I loved that work — every assignment I took on was treatment-oriented. In many ways, I was being trained as a therapist long before I had the title.

But over the years, I saw so much pain — so many people hurting silently, disconnected from hope or help. I couldn't ignore it. That's what led me to go back to school to become a therapist. I wanted to break the stigma surrounding mental health, especially within the African American community.

While pursuing my master's degree in psychology, my father passed away. As part of my program requirements, I had to complete twenty hours of personal therapy. I figured I'd "get it out of the way" — but it became one of the most transformative experiences of my life.

I engaged in grief therapy, both individual and group. I went in thinking I was fine, functioning, and productive. What I discovered was that I was deeply depressed — hiding behind work and academics. That process broke me open in the best way.

I graduated summa cum laude with my Master of Science in Psychology. By then, I had developed the ability to look past the pain and anger, to see the story beneath the struggle to help others heal.

Let's be honest, I was the only one in my entire family who had ever gone to therapy, but your past does not determine your future. Despite being raised with a lack of awareness and access to the power of therapy, I knew *this was what I was called to do.*

Today, I am a proud mother of three and grandmother of four. I often look back and smile, knowing that every challenge I faced shaped the woman I've become. Therapy was the missing link I needed to truly understand and manage the symptoms I carried from life's events — pain I didn't even realize was sitting beneath the surface. It gave me language for my experience, peace in my heart, and a renewed sense of purpose.

Now, I attend New Life Christian Church, where I volunteer with our mental health ministry. I host monthly Zoom classes and counsel individuals who need support. I know without a doubt that God has His hand on the work I do — because, in my own strength, none of this would have been possible.

Providing a space where people can be vulnerable, learn to manage life, and begin to heal — that's my dream. And I wouldn't have it any other way.

# Healing Begins When You Invite God into the Garden of Your Mind

by Pastor Tamika Casey

There was a season in my life when I prayed for God to heal everything around me, yet the real work He desired was within me. I learned that while I was faithfully tending to ministry, marriage, motherhood, and the women God entrusted to my care, the garden of my own mind had places that needed His touch. There were thoughts that had grown wild, emotions I had buried, and weary places I had never permitted myself to rest in.

As a Christian woman and as a pastor, I once believed that mental and emotional struggles were things to "press through" or "pray away." But the Holy Spirit gently showed me that healing begins not with pretending we are strong, but with inviting God into the quiet, tender places of our inner world. It is there — in the soil of our thoughts, feelings, and memories — that the Master Gardener does His most transformative work.

Reading *The Garden Within* by Dr. Anita Phillips reminded me that God cares deeply about the landscape of our minds. He designed us as integrated beings — spirit, soul, and body — and He desires that each part of us flourishes. Mental wellness is not separate from our faith; it is a part of the abundant life Jesus promised. When we tend our internal garden with God, we invite Him to plant peace where there was anxiety, joy where there was heaviness, and hope where there was despair.

Scripture affirms this truth. *Beloved, I wish above all things that thou mayest prosper and be in health, even as thy soul prospereth* (3 John 1:2). God desires not just spiritual salvation for us but emotional wellness, mental clarity, and inner peace. He is concerned with the state of our soul — the very seat of our emotions and thoughts.

There came a moment when I had to be honest with God about the frustrations, fears, anxieties, and heaviness I carried. And in that moment of honesty, I felt the peace that surpasses understanding settle over me. It wasn't the peace that comes from ignoring pain or pretending to be strong — it was the peace that grows when we let God pull out the weeds, prune what is overgrown, and plant seeds of healing.

I've learned that prayer and therapy can coexist. Rest and worship can walk hand in hand. Silence can be as holy as a shout. God uses counselors, doctors, and mental health professionals just as He uses pastors, prophets, and teachers. Healing is holistic because God is holistic.

To everyone reading this: Your mind matters to God. Your emotional health matters to God. Your story, your wounds, and your healing are all part of the testimony He is writing through your life. You do not have to choose between faith and wellness. You can tend your inner garden with Scripture in one hand and support in the other.

# Piece by Peace

by Naysha Coker

Inspired by a Peer Support Specialist graduation. During the ceremony, the instructors described the therapy process as akin to the Japanese art of Kintsugi – mending after traumatic experiences. Each poem was written through the lens of therapeutic healing steps, reflecting the emotional and spiritual process of trauma recovery and restoration.

PART 1 — At 1st Fracture

Every porcelain piece put on display,
a vision made apparent in disarray.

In humility you dare to touch healing,
realizing brokenness itself is treasure.

Instead of hiding what's undone,
you begin step one.

Take inventory of a fractured vessel,
noting each experience with careful curiosity,
capturing each piece not to magnify a single shard
but to sand down sharp edges—

finding symmetry
within the pieces of a person.

And before I'm even aware,
I've cast all of my cares
like an answered prayer.

---

PART 2 — Reclaim, Name, and Repair

On hands and knees,
I'm seeking the highest hand
to mend my affliction.

In step two, You'll replenish every blue dereliction.

I know You hold the tools
to make grief glisten like gold.

Sort my feelings, gather my memories,
and reclaim my history
all in the palm of Your hand.

Like lacquer,
I know You'll fill the holes
of every disaster.

---

PART 3 — Holy Union

With me in mind,
You redefine beauty.

In step three we'll see,
a newfound truth — a marriage of marred pieces.

Every softened edge,
a full-fledged commitment.

Because we broke the mold together,
we behold grace.

Share our space,
separate our peace from past,
release our need
to fill every hole perfect.

---

PART 4 — The Potter's Hand

Joined side by side,
a seam becomes a star,
a scar becomes a story,
and healing reveals God's glory.

Bound by a lacquer —
in step four gold shines
between every disaster.

Even while being preserved,
porcelain is still porcelain
to the Potter.

That same hand knew
that I, an engaged, changed,
and visible person,
was only a piece of porcelain.

---

PART 5 — Claim an Issue Find an Amen

What a privilege
for porcelain
to bear a problem.

Through patience
each piece
connects with the divine
in peace.

This is Kintsugi

Isaiah 64:8

# Faith and Mental Health: Discussion Questions

Use these questions to spark conversation about the poems, stories, and essays in this section.

## Exploring Black Mental Health Through a Christian Lens

by Pastor Samuel J. Casey

1. In this essay, three examples of people dealing with a mental health crisis find relief based on their needs and "treatment." Do you think these examples are relatable? Can you think of others from scripture? Do you find this relevant to your own life?

2. It seems more pastors and ministers are embracing the services offered by mental health practitioners. What do you think has brought about this change in the church?

3. While the focus is on the Black church and Christianity, there are many religions where faith and mental health have integral roles. Think about other religions and their relationship with mental health. Are they similar or different from Christianity?

4. How do those religions approach mental health now?

5. The photo following the essay is of people in a church. Mental illness is often an invisible struggle. How can leaders and people in places of worship create an environment where we praise the Lord and also feel comfortable admitting the need for mental and emotional help?

---

## Neurodivergent

by Jay Writes

1. What ADHD symptoms frustrate the poet?

2. The poet is upset about having an ADHD diagnosis and decides that if he can love others, he can learn to love his own mind. The poem ends with that declaration. What are some of the ways you think the poet could learn to accept or love his own mind?

3. Does he acknowledge any positive symptoms from ADHD? Do you know of any positive qualities? (See resources under **Faith & Mental Health**, near the end of the book, for more information.)

---

## Resurrection by Alexander James, Depression by Lydia Theon Ware i, Chaos by Marcus Thompson, and What the Preacher Said by Anjetta (Anjie) Williams

1. The people in these poems are wrestling with varying degrees of depression, from loneliness to suicidal ideation. Sorrow is part of the human condition. What do you think the difference is between a bout of sadness and depression? (See resources under **Faith & Mental Health**, near the end of the book, for more information).

---

## Daily Meds
by Alora Young

1. What does the photo *Daily Meds* by Alora Young say about the person in the photo and their attitude about medication? What commentary do you think she is making about faith and belief?

## Reclaiming My "No"
by Dr. Ahliah Sharp

1. What are the dynamics of this abusive relationship?

2. Why did the speaker in the poem stay in the relationship?

3. What helped her to "reclaim her no?"

---

## What I Discovered
by Tona Farlow

1. What surprised you about the person in this story?

2. What did you find most inspirational about her journey?

## Healing Begins When You Invite God into the Garden of Your Mind

by Pastor Tamika Casey

1. In the pastor's testimony, she gives a snapshot of her life where she used to try to "press through" or "pray away" her struggles. She then informs us that, " ... *the Holy Spirit gently showed me that healing begins not with pretending we are strong, but with inviting God into the quiet, tender places of our inner world.* Do you think this supports or contradicts the bible? Why/why not?

2. In the fourth paragraph of this essay, the pastor uses scripture to support her claim that *God desires not only spiritual salvation for us but also emotional wellness, mental clarity, and inner peace.* In the sixth paragraph, she tells us: *God uses counselors, doctors, and mental health professionals just as He uses pastors, prophets, and teachers.* Despite the use of scripture, some believers think mental illness is only a matter of spiritual oppression and possession and suggest there has not been enough fasting and praying. They believe there is a lack of faith, and they find scripture to support their position, even though reality might not. What is your view on mental health, salvation, and faith? Why do you have this perspective?

---

## Piece by Peace

by Naysha Coker

1. This five-part poem describes a process of healing trauma in body and spirit. Discuss what you think the poet is describing and the result.

# Have you had a mental health check-up lately?

by Romaine Washington

"You go for a yearly physical for your body. You should also have a mental health checkup for your mental wellness." A presenter in the Healthy Heritage: Broken Crayons Still Color educational series on Black mental health encouraged us. And it makes perfect sense to me. Our body chemistry and hormones are constantly changing and that impacts how we feel and think. You can look for online resources and do a checkup to make sure you have the necessary resources and strategies for wellness.

From another source I learned that you do not need to be in a life-or-death crisis to seek help. You do not need to be in unbearable pain. In *My Grandmother's Hands: Racialized Trauma and the Mending of Our Bodies and Hearts*, Resmaa Menakem explains, "In today's America, we tend to think of healing as something binary: either we're broken or we're healed from that brokenness. But that's not how healing operates, and it's almost never how human growth works. More often, **healing and growth take place on a continuum, with innumerable points between utter brokenness and total health.**"

**Self-care** doesn't always come naturally. and it is easy to get out of balance. Here are eight different areas for self-care to help build routine and balance on the wellness continuum. If you need help, this will guide you to pinpoint what you need to do and where you might go for advice.

**Ask yourself: How am I caring for myself in these areas?**

- **Emotional** (gratitude, triggers)
- **Mental** (self-talk, mindfulness)
- **Intellectual** (learning, reading)
- **Physical** (nutrition, exercise, sleep/rest)
- **Environment** (clean, organized)
- **Social** (friendships, hobbies, boundaries)
- **Spiritual** (nature, prayer/meditation, depends on the person)
- **Financial** (budget, income and expenses)
- I am adding an extra domain. **Technology** (Do you feel you have a balance with your (IRL) "in real life" experiences and your online experiences? Do you trust yourself to write your own papers, create your own art, explore questions you don't know the answer to without technology? How important is it to you?

Samantha Cooper. Counseling Today: Mental Health Care Stigma in Black Communities. (Feb. 2023). April 26, 2026. https://www.counseling.org/publications/counseling-today-magazine/article-archive/article/legacy/mental-health-care-stigma-in-black-communities

# Mind and Body Wisdom

You were not just born
to center your entire existence
on work and labor.
You were born to heal, to grow,
to be of service to yourself and community,
to practice, to experiment, to create,
to have space, to dream, and to connect.

– Tricia Hersey,
Rest is Resistance: A Manifesto

# Acolytes

by Ellen June Wright

I watch them    the people
    with their heads bowed

as if in prayer    hands
    as if holding a prayer book

but when I look closely
    it's a different god they worship

without knowing
    they have become acolytes

to the god of technology
    and paid for the privilege

an offering into the hundreds
    or thousands    and they would give

their lives:    walk into traffic
    into signposts  into ditches

open manholes    never looking up
    from their *studies*    enthralled

by whatever deity    lives in their palms

# Organs to the System: Lessons from Fibroid Removal Surgery

by Violeta Antone

It's hard to remember
not every ounce of energy gained
has to be spent.

It's hard not to spend
that hard-earned energy on work,
or thoughts about work.

It's hard to remember
that the medical recommendation
to lift no more than fifteen pounds

the first two weeks post-op
includes your twenty-something pounds
amazing kid.

In hubris, it's hard to remember
this one strong body you have
is fragile flesh, vulnerable

to benign tumors, poor air quality,
and the strain of a short walk
to the nearby toddler park.

If there's no practice,
it's hard to remember
which order to take your medications

when you think you are clear-headed.
It's hard to remember post-surgery
you may feel better than you actually are.

When does practice come in?
Does it come in before or after
your life-changing event?

When do you remember
hubris has done everything

from kicking seventeen million off Medicaid,

to revoking USAID,
instigating wars,
and believing in our crumbling empire,
*We'll survive*?

With whom do you practice
shedding your hubris?

Let me settle into this here flesh and rest.
Let my energy be used for its right purposes.
May I not use it frivolously.

May my bladder and intestines,
lower back and hips, uterus and bowels
be given unrestricted funds of resolve

to care for themselves and the system.
May resources be reallocated
in interest of the highest priority

of this here recovering body.
May I thank my organs with the same fervor
that I show up in church

saying "Thanks be to God."
May I thank this glorious body
given to me by the Creator

and treat it as the precious,
fragile rarity that it is.
May my lungs breathe

with emoción like a petition
from a Mojuba prayer.
May my temptations

to do just a little too much
be mediated so that this here body
has the power to heal.

*Mojuba – African traditional religious prayer.

# In My Mind, Not My Heart

by Nia Crawford

When you visit the doctor, you are asked to arrive fifteen minutes early to update your personal information. Today, I check different boxes on those forms while some stay the same.

1. Any allergies? Check
2. Explain #1. Penicillin. Anaphylactic Shock.
3. Family history of heart disease? Check.
4. Explain #3. Father was a candidate for a heart transplant.
5. Have you had major surgery or open-heart surgery? Check. July 14, 2015
6. Do your mitral valve leaflets flop their way through heartbeats like the swinging door in a restaurant kitchen? Not anymore.

The valve leaflets don't close tightly like the vault door at a Wells Fargo branch, but the situation is much better than before. Pre-surgery, the bad valve not only leaked blood but also caused a backflow that pounded my heart wall. Think eroded sea wall.

That's why I got mitral valve repair surgery on a hot, humid day at Philadelphia's Penn Presbyterian Hospital in July 2015.

Leading up to the surgery was a journey. I had never spent one night in the hospital, let alone a whole week. But my father had, and I had bad memories of his hospital stays, which were unplanned and unwanted. The food was the least of his worries; he was a very sick man.

I did not realize it then, but I was becoming a very anxious teenager who was cracking under the strain of caring for an ailing parent, whose jovial spirit and quick intellect masked his illness many times.

Looking back, I see my own journey that encapsulates my open-heart surgery. It's recounted below.

**May 2015**

When I visited my cardiologist, Dr. Carter, for my yearly exam, he said I was sick and needed surgery.

When I told friends about my upcoming surgery, most of them asked, "How'd you get sick?"

Sick people take medication. They feel bad. When I looked in the mirror, a 42-year-old woman who jogged half-marathons stared back.

*I am not sick. I just need surgery.*

**June 2015**

My friends also wanted to know if my surgery was the same surgery my dad needed.

My father, who had a diseased heart, enlarged liver, and porous lungs, died one June morning in 1993. When my sister went downstairs to drive him to his weekly treatments at the local hospital, she found him lying on the floor. He was fifty-four years old.

*Nope, my dad needed a heart transplant. I just need a week in the hospital. A very ad hoc situation.*

**July 12-13, 2015**

Days before the surgery, it hurt to walk or sit up straight. I went to the local emergency room, secretly hoping that I'd be diagnosed with some illness that would postpone my surgery. All I did was rack up more medical bills.

When the emergency room doctor asked me the reason for my visit, I should have told her *I'm here because anxiety is a liar*!

**July 14, 2015**

My mom took me to the hospital at the time bakers are headed to work to knead dough. Once I was checked in, I showered with a special antibacterial soap, dressed for the occasion, and hopped onto the gurney. They wheeled me to a small room that quickly became crowded. The anesthesiologist asked me to count down, and then it was lights out.

When I awoke, I was confused, but I quickly realized I could not talk because a tube was stuffed down my throat. The nurses warned me they would remove it, but they did not tell me it would hurt. Later that day, the nurses removed tubes from my neck and my chest.

Each one hurt more than the other. All the nurses had to do was *let a girl* know that yanking tubes from a person's body was gonna hurt like hell.

**July 16, 2015**

After two days in the ICU, it was time to move to cardiac care. In the hallway, I saw a patient lying on a gurney with tubes everywhere. Nurses surrounded her, and one held a balloon over her face, pushing it.

I asked the nurse who was wheeling me to my new unit if I looked like that when I came to the ICU. When he said "Yup," I told him to *push me a little faster*.

**July 20, 2015**

On the sixth day in the hospital, my cardiologist told me that if I stayed in the hospital any longer, I risked getting sick. There goes Dr. Carter lying to me again.

That was doctor talk for you need to get the hell out of this hospital. The water pills got me down to my pre-op weight, and I was walking on my own.

What Dr. Carter didn't know is that I couldn't sleep unless someone was nearby, I jumped every time I heard a machine beep, and I burst into tears the first few times the nurses encouraged me to walk down the hall. I flat-out told them I couldn't do it.

Dr. Carter also didn't know his warning fell flat on a freshly repaired heart valve and an anxious mind. To his warning, "You risk getting sick if you stay in the hospital," I should have replied, *It don't matter; I'm already sick*.

**July 20—Aug 10, 2015**

I went from the hospital to my sister's couch. There, I barely moved for three weeks. I refused to go outside. The heat would kill me. I refused to shave my armpits, get a manicure, or a haircut.

A little cut would kill me now that I was on blood thinners. I refused to shower unless someone was in the house. I'd fall and hit my head.

Every morning, when my sister asked if she'd see me in the same spot on the couch when she returned home from work, I stuck out my chest and said, "Yup."

If I understood my symptoms, I would have explained that the debilitating anxiety I experienced as a teenager when I took care of my sick father was back. *It hijacked my healing.*

**August 2015**

As the dog days of summer persisted, it hit me that the weather wasn't going to change, and neither would my healing if I did not do something. On a Wednesday, I spent all day mustering the courage to open the front door and walk outside. I didn't even bother to close the door because if I made it off the porch, down the steps to the sidewalk, I wouldn't move past that point. I walked down the concrete steps one at a time. Then I used the same slow-but-steady movement to walk down the sidewalk. About fifty feet later, I reached the corner and made a quick decision to keep going. One hundred feet later, I reached an intersection. I marveled at my accomplishment before I began to walk back. In the next block, I saw my sister in front of her house, looking up and down the street. I knew she had just arrived home from work and was looking for me. I yelled her name and waved my hand, and she began to run to me. When she was close enough, she hugged me and told me how proud she was of me. I smiled and said, Oh, *I decided to take a little walk.*

**May 2016**

The months passed, and I got a grip on my anxiety. I began to understand it, deconstruct it, and reject the lies that fueled it. Family helped. So did friends. One friend, who is also a personal trainer and the fittest friend I have, offered to run Philadelphia's 10-mile Broad Street Run with me. The annual race starts at the hospital where I was born. It passes my high school football field and the college where I earned a bachelor's and master's degree. It ends at the Navy Yard, which is steps from the sports stadium where the Rocky statue lived for years.

That rainy first Sunday in May, we lined up with 40,000 other runners to conquer Philadelphia's longest street. I felt the pulse of the Rocky theme music and Survivor's "Eye of the Tiger" blasting through the speakers. As I prepared to cross the starting line and inch my way toward the finish line, I thought about the *eye of the tiger* and the "thrill of the fight." This fight was going to be a good one, but not a new one. I completed the Broad Street Run five times in previous years, but this time was the first after heart surgery. The thrill, the runner's high, should hit by mile 3. I was hungry for it.

I felt tall knowing I had not only risen "up to the challenge of my rival" but damn near obliterated the anxiety that crippled me months ago.

I looked at my friend and asked her if she was ready. In that instance, we decided there'd be no "you run your race, I'll run mine"; we decided to run, not walk, the whole race. Together. The eyes of two tigers facing one fight.

# She Lives Always Seeking the Silver Lining: Mental Health Challenges and Triumphs living with Sickle Cell Disease

by Sheila Louise Bennett Marchbanks, aka She-She

**I.**

Living with Sickle Cell Disease (SCD) can impact every aspect of one's life. Sickle Cell is an inherited genetic condition that affects the red blood cells and may present many complex health complications throughout the life of an individual born with the disease. The hallmark burden that accompanies this condition is PAIN.

PAIN that is felt in the body and, for many, also in the mind. The PAIN, which can be acute and chronic, has a far-reaching impact on the physical and mental life of a Sickle Cell Warrior. You may ask, just how does a blood disease impact the mind?

As blood circulates throughout the body, this flow supports life. In contrast, as a result of SCD, with the lack of adequate blood flow, naturally, there is a compromised flow of life. This diminished flow of the life-giving blood contributes to the experience of PAIN, which I characterize and experience as a direct assault on life.

In essence, the breakdown does not bring life; the repeated occurrences can slowly (or suddenly) erode the life of affected organs in the physical body, and being more than physical beings, may also impact the mental health and wellness of the Sickle Cell Disease Warrior.

An SCD Warrior's battle with PAIN, which is commonly referred to as an SCD Crisis, may range from the existence of a hovering overhead dark cloud full of knowing, remembering, and dreading to actually going through the anguish, the dark clouds release, and unbearable rain.

My wonderful Shero and Mentor, Retired Nurse Pat Corley, says, "Warriors are born to Pain." And I say, amen, PAIN that sometimes makes me think my brain is going to explode or fly away!

After the dark cloud and the rain, where visible and invisible damage may have been done, there is a need for time for recovery, regrouping, and hopefully regaining as much as possible that which was affected by the SCD PAIN Crisis. This loop, this pattern, this cycle of interruptions to life, coping with all of the complexities (it would take a book to explain) wears on the mind, especially over time...This too shall pass, this cloud has a silver lining, it's a promise I've lived to attest!

So, having outlets to address the whole human being, which incorporates the essential mental health component, is foundational to achieving a more vibrant, balanced, whole life.

Until Covid-19, during the 2020-2023 era, mental health was not too cool to talk about, to access, to acknowledge, let alone to seek and to utilize in general and even less so in the African-American community. Since then, I have heard more Warriors talking openly and positively about considering, seeking, obtaining, benefiting, sustaining, and referring others to mental health services. A huge step forward in wrap-around health care.

Well, it's a new day, a silver lining of Covid-19, is that some of the African-American historically and culturally bound shame and stigma and 'denial of need' have dissipated, a breakthrough in the clouds, glory Halleluiah, it's a brighter and new day!! Please come along with me as I share a short vignette.

## II.

A bright and sunny day, life is good, and I'm on my way. Not one cloud, I can say. The wind hits me. Hmmm, a tapping sensation starts in my bones, gentle at first, then an increasing thump, a message that I don't want to hear is speaking oh so clearly in my ear. No, no, please not today. I have plans, meeting friends, bought tickets, got a babysitter, and am looking cute too!

As I get out of my car, I start to limp; the pain has now escalated to the point that it's difficult to navigate up the stairs, but I made it. Well, it looks like I will have to again turn back around and miss out on another planned Sistah-Friend Days Trip.

At this point, I wonder how long this Sickle Cell Crisis will last. My mind is on getting adequate pain relief, getting into some hot water, and praying that this pain does not spike upward, that this doesn't linger on and on for many hours, for days, or for weeks.

All of these prayers are also coupled with the fear of what the worst could be. So, once the pain has tapered down somewhat, my emotions, you know, the truth of my feelings surface. I am sad and disappointed to have missed the event of the day. There are small proportionate measures of loss that also contribute to the totality of my depressed feelings, including: the money loss, the fun-time loss, the get-away from home loss, and the pseudo-sense of being SCD-Free loss.

## III.

Throughout my life, these interruptions, though not the 'end of the world, do cause another type of pain. After repeated occurrences of SCD Crisis over the course of my life, I have noticed that a form of hesitancy or overprotectiveness, or extreme cautiousness has periodically crept into my mind, impacted my behavior.

For instance, some family and friends have said, "Oh Sheila, you're doing/asking too much", "you don't have to be so cautious", "don't worry about being exposed to...". Whether or not these thoughts and actions are rational or balanced, I'm not entirely sure. Having to live one's life on guard can wear you down a bit. Having to encounter repeated pain episodes, recovery periods, picking up, and catching up can be wearying.

For instance, typical environments such as exposure to wind, variable temperature changes, and common colds can be severe triggers and knock me to my knees, whereby I may be down for up to a month, having been exposed to these triggers and getting 'sick'. Living with SCD, having this compromised immune system, hyper-vigilance, and sensitivity becomes a constant companion, somewhat like preemptive bodyguards.

Stress, an ever-present reality for most, is a heightened factor, a significant trigger that has to be reckoned with on so many planes. As a Warrior, I know that my health challenges impact many areas of my life and the lives of my immediate family members and some of my friends.

Yes, our health challenges reach far beyond impacting one's family and friends; caregivers, co-workers, careers, education, and finances are other entities whereby another layer of heaviness may be carried as a burden for the Warrior. This again is a whole other story in and of itself.

As a result, the Warrior may live with guilt or feel responsible to backfill the losses, the contributions, and the sacrifices that others have made for them. So when the Warrior is well, or well enough, they may try to overcompensate. And guess what, exacerbating physical, emotional, psychological, and/or mental overload.

With the cognition of these risks, with the help of good health care, with the support of loved ones, and with the counseling from professional providers and personal confidantes, the SCD Warrior can build the skills to realize their best physical and mental life. I know this to be true, because I DO!

## IV.

Believe Me, Believe Us

Believe me, why don't they believe me!?
What do I have to do? What do I have to say so that I don't crack?
The raging in my body is beyond any word called PAIN!
Insane
My PAIN Plan is in My Chart.
Please use it. Consult it, please let's start.

The cycle continues, and we're still not believed.
Too many times, we're
Gnarled painfully in fetal positions
Tears searing our skin and souls
Half a dose of meds, they say.
In the midst, our bodies and brains
Feel like they are gonna explode!
Makes us cry out to Go!    No, No, No!!

Believe Me, Believe Us!
Warriors strongly bounce back and say:
We believe in our Creator.
We believe in our Calling.
We believe in our Community.

## Mode of Support

Model and Photographer: Alora Young

## The Five Stages
by Dr. Ahliah Sharp

*How did I feel about the news?*

Mom, I remember you coming to my job with Dad. I knew you had a doctor's appointment that day and had been waiting to hear what happened, but I never expected you to come to my job. I knew when I saw you both that it was bad news.

*As a therapist, I know grief comes in stages, and death does not have to be the reason that grief introduces itself. Not everyone goes through the stages in the same order, but this is how I felt.*

**Stage One** —Denial

You both looked calm and disturbed at the same time. You told me the news, "It's cancer." I completely lost it. It didn't make sense to me, and I thought there was absolutely *no way* this could be true. No way! You are too calm; it cannot be true, but there's no way you both would prank me with something so serious.

Here you were, with *the news*, trying to comfort *me*. I couldn't catch my breath. I cannot remember anything else about that day. But what I do remember is everything else.

How were you so calm? I remember that you had decided to have elective surgery before hearing *the news*, and one of your questions was whether this would affect your ability to have *that* surgery. I couldn't help but think you lost it, cuz mom, where were your priorities?

**Stage Two** —Anger

I was extremely angry at you for being so calm. How selfish is that? Do you remember that conversation we had about you being more animated about a nail breaking than your cancer diagnosis? You said you learned a long time ago to give the big things to God, but clearly, I wasn't there yet.

I wasn't just angry with you, Mom; I was angry with you, too, Dad, for taking so much on yourself. I was angry with my brother for being in the Navy and not close enough to have to see and experience the day-to-day. I was angry with my grandmother for being killed a few years prior, because I just believed in my perfect imaginary world, she would have come to stay with us and been there for you like only a mom can.

On top of being angry, I was paranoid. This is the part I don't want to confess. I don't want to sound like I was insensitive to you, battling this horrible disease. I don't want it to seem like I was trivializing it. But you asked me about my coping strategies. This is genuinely what I had to do.

**Stage Three** —Depression

Before I came to terms with it all, I was a wreck. I checked my breasts daily, several times a day. You always said you felt your lump one day, not the day before. So, I convinced myself that I had to check often to avoid the same result. Here I am, 28 and having to go through what most don't have to experience until their 40s. Still, my medical history now reads maternal risk for breast cancer.

One Sunday, I was convinced I felt something. I saw the nurse, Deaconess Magby, in church, so I grabbed her and pulled her into the side bathroom and literally had her feel my breasts in the bathroom before church. I was so hysterical, I couldn't eat or sleep well. She gave me the reassurance I needed at that moment, but I knew I had to do something to shake this. Yes, I tried praying and all of that. Please don't think I don't know where my peace comes from, but at that moment, at that time in my life, it just didn't seem like enough. Again, I am just being fully transparent.

*Now, the part I don't want to share...*

**Stage Four** —Bargaining

One day I just couldn't breathe, I couldn't think, I couldn't focus. It was consuming me. Finally, I said to myself, I have always wanted full breasts; if I do end up with this diagnosis, I'll get *real breasts*. I realized that it is *not* how I should view this. I know it is *not* as simple as breast surgery. Breast cancer is not an elective procedure.

I was not in a good place, and going through that thought process helped me to move into a better headspace. I understand how insulting my thought process sounds, and now as a psychologist, I realize our battles are our battles. We have to do what we have to do to get through them as whole as possible.

**Stage Five** —Acceptance

Once I took the power of fear away, I stopped being angry with you, Mom, and started being impressed with your unwavering faith. Usually, anyone just had to give you half a reason to take the day off work. You were good with it, but here you were going to work while losing your hair and having chemo and radiation treatments. It didn't make sense to me, but that was when I truly started to gain a better, more intimate relationship with God. Watching you destroy your diagnosis and show no fear at all was more than admirable, and I am so proud of you.

Note: When someone you love gets a diagnosis, it attacks us all in different ways. Nobody really cares how you are feeling or handling it; it isn't your diagnosis after all. But let me be the first to tell you, you matter too. You need not be afraid to talk with someone about your fears and your struggles. Get help, don't do like I did and suffer in silence. I did it to myself, and it was not necessary. Yes, it is *their* battle, but the residue of war bleeds on our loved ones.

# Diagnosing It

by Carmen Estela Kennedy Saleh

Mrs. R. M. Hall never ceased to leverage her status as the Colonel's wife; never failed to mention she was educated; never fell into formation with the women of her time. She left the NCO's wives agog, guessing at her practiced affectations. She bleached her hair and hit her kitchen with a hot comb so none would be the wiser. She wore a shade of frosted lipstick to complement what they mistook as a year-round tan. Mrs. Hall was indeed the lady.

She had a choice table at the Officer's Club and a highball, or perhaps two, the afternoon her car grazed the median before exiting the base, the peach-faced MP apologized before asking to see her ID. He would grasp the tip of his cap with his thumb and forefinger upon seeing that her vehicle was registered to an officer. And she would ease her shoulders, sliding her hands into a ten and two o'clock position, wondering if her charm had eclipsed her race on occasions like this. She would wonder whether this was a remnant of the boundaries that blurred her image of herself as the officer's wife and of who she was behind her pretenses. Perhaps it was her ersatz existence in this hierarchical structure that made her scream.

We didn't know how to describe it. Is it that she was upset, agitated, apoplectic, agonized by an affliction we could not name? Our eyes, wild and aphasic, watched her in silence as she assaulted us, my dad and me, with high-pitched screams.

Looking back, I suppose it was the symptom of a terrible thing that went undiagnosed. A diagnosis could have brought us peace, closure, and an opportunity to box, name, and understand it to the extent we could have gotten her help. But that never happened. It makes me wonder if she is still screaming at this moment.

• • •

I was born in 1961. I was eventually told that my mother had what Dad would call a breakdown. It is not a breakdown, as it does not describe what happened, what continues to happen. And yet, as I do not have the words to explain my mother's behavior, I'm guessing it has something to do with me. Perhaps I provoke it; I mean, perhaps I'm responsible for her unleashing these guttural screams.

This was, ***this is***, confusing. I wanted my dad to explain these occurrences to me, but I did not ask him, or perhaps I could not. And the years passed.

I gathered that, *the sum of it was, more than anything, he survived*, from his point of entry–the silent generation–to his military service and subsequent life as a civilian, and where he is, for me, in memory.

He swaddles me in a blanket, whispering, "This will soon pass."

In a disquieting dream or faded memory of mine, my dad would have loosened his hold as the open arms of a trusted neighbor enveloped me. It would have been hard for him to call upon them, but he would have been grateful for their support and discretion. He would have opened the car door and watched my mother fold herself into the seat. She would have done this without a word, as there would have been nothing to say at that point. If he had turned on the radio, then Sarah Vaughn would have brought a welcome distraction from the thoughts that were making his headache. Her dulcet tones would have carried them along the road to the hospital, the mental institution, the funny farm, which would have taken an oxymoronic turn as a somber staff member would have greeted my mother and induced for her an otherwise elusive calm.

My mother's visit would not have lasted long, as anything beyond a couple of days would have been impossible to keep under wraps. And there would have been a concerted effort to wrap her situation in full opacity, in ways that clamored to see the light of day. I should have asked my dad more, but I did not know his silence was trying to say everything he had been struggling to voice.

•••

She would never scream or carry on in public. She would never set aside social graces in the presence of others. And she would never put her business in the street. After all, Mrs. Hall was a lady, and as such, she knew where and when to behave like one. And as this was the case, she must have been in control, and if so, why would she intentionally plague our lives and our quiet home with her vituperative screams?

"Ma!"

I remember the early school version of myself pleading, hands clasped against the sides of my head, wondering why she could not see me or the tissue balled up in my fist like a white flag.

•••

In the 70s, every room, except mine, had an ashtray.

Valium, a.k.a. "mother's little helper," belonged to a class of burgeoning psychopharmaceuticals that were prescribed unreservedly to quiet the niggling physiological and behavioral issues of women. Many of these women dealt with overlapping issues, only to be treated with dismissal and dope. But there was nothing niggling about my mother's neuroses; that is, whatever pain or malevolence she thought she was experiencing, even if it began and ended in her mind, was real enough to warrant relief. And relief she sought, chasing down prescriptions with a highball, easing into a pack of Viceroy, or losing herself in a bottle of J&B.

For more than a decade of my life, spirits for her were sine qua non, and as her junior confidant, I never asked why she had no qualms about conscripting me as her barkeep. A breakfast Bloody Mary with its bright celery greens gasping at the rim of a glass. Scotch and soda on the rocks, reflections on the tinkling sound of ice in a glass of piss colored liquor. An olive impaled with its mouth agape, drowning in a chilled martini, and pouring from its pimento heart is the confounding declaration, "Mother, I love you."

•••

My mother is upstairs in her room. She is slumped over on the side of her bed, head in her hands, and again she has been screaming. It would be impossible to explain to someone what goes on with her when she is having these episodes, as impossible as capturing fairies in a jar. Who would believe it? Especially when she maintains the illusion of a perfectly ordered life. This evening, however, her untoward behavior is more than enough to prompt my dad to reach out to someone for help.

I turned twelve recently, and her behavior is more of a curiosity to me than a frightful thing now. But I still want her to get diagnosed.

Schmidt is a neighbor who lives a couple of doors down from us. He happens to be a doctor. His diplomas and certificates hang in his study, and his study is a spectacle of his pride and privilege. He's proud of his house and his cute little cabriolet. And he's proud of his wife, who is not last on this list to her diminution, but because Schmidt's priorities are, even to the preadolescent me, kind of misplaced.

I liked Schmidt's wife, inasmuch as a kid might like their adult neighbors. She was a bit of a Gidget, a dishwater blonde with expensive, prêt-à-porter taste. She gave me a few of her hand-me-downs. I thanked her and waited to be alone to examine the fine fabric and French seams. The styles suited me and my middle school frame, and my quirky aesthetic: blouses with Peter Pan collars, turtlenecks, and smart little minis, mod shifts in St. John-like knits. I even kept one that to this day has never pilled. So, Schmidt's wife simply outclassed him, in my opinion.

It was a little after sundown, and Schmidt grabbed his bag on the way out the door. He crossed over the neighbor's yard and caught up with my dad. Both entered our house and bounded up the stairs to the second floor. The door to my mother's bedroom was ajar. A three-way bulb in the lamp beside her bed shone bright, uncomfortably so. It cast her in silhouette, and I found it hard to look directly at her with the light in that position, so I kept my distance, standing in the hallway.

In a scene that could only be described as kabuki theatre: the overly expressive countenance, the character interplay, the imaginary wail of a Shinobu, and a superfluous prop: a stethoscope, Schmidt began his performance.

"Hey Ann. Hey, hey, what's going on?"

Her lips quivering as he crouched beside her. She would stop the chanting she had reserved for only dad and me. She would hiccup, mutter her last, "Miss my mama," and not speak anymore of the dead.

"I can't." She would sigh and collapse back onto her pillow.

"Ann, what's going on?"

I was no doctor, but I was sure that asking this in any sense other than rhetorical, of someone who was hysterical, was absurd. Schmidt must have known my mother was not going to make this easy or quicken a diagnosis. He could not coax her from a sunken place if the sinkhole was her go-to, couldn't apply consonance to a situation born out of dissonance. And could not determine a damn thing with the few minutes he and his silly stethoscope had given her. So, my hope of a diagnosis disappeared the minute it was clear that Schmidt didn't know what the hell he was doing.

And then he quit. He could not diagnose my mother. But he was confident enough to say she was depressed.

*No shit.*

He would have the audacity to imply that her depression was the result of something my father had done, or in this case, had not done enough; my dad had not let her run us over enough, not yielded to her demands enough, not fallen prey to her manipulations enough, and not known when enough was enough.

Schmidt, with dubious medicalese, would offer her a sedative. "It'll help her rest." He was stymied by whatever was ailing my mother, but was it an ailment?

Regardless of what it was, she deserved an examiner with the know-how and stamina to sort her out. This was not Schmidt. He struck me as the type who would never have to put much work into anything. Okay. So, he was a doctor, evidenced by his diploma: a piece of paper that could not show how good, or in this case maladroit, he was at doctoring; as Ann was my mother, but could not defend how good or not she was at mothering; semantics like these plagued our mother/daughter relationship.

Weeks passed. Schmidt and his little wife looked at us differently. There would be no more hand-me-downs. Their ebullient hello-and-how-are-you would eventually fade into the infrequent reserved nod.

My dad took a leap of faith that night, bringing someone in from the outside. He must have been terribly desperate when he decided to do it. It was a thing he would try once and never again.

•••

It was 1975.

We had moved to the Northern California Bay Area. Wooden shingles were having an architectural heyday. The roof and façade of our tract home were covered in them. Still, they were a fire hazard that ultimately sparked environmental and political problems for the state. Eventually, they were banned, as were other flammables like rayon pajamas and the aerosol hair spray my mother wore while drifting off, a cigarette in one hand, a glass of scotch in the other.

One day, latched to the base of her neck was a goiter that became distended with stress and hormones to the extent she couldn't take another drag. And she quit cold turkey. Women are up to eight times more likely to suffer from a thyroid condition than men. These conditions can be more than just uncomfortable, indeed quite serious, prompting anything from thyroiditis, Graves', and heart disease to cancer if untreated. My mother, left with her condition for some time, might have been heading toward the latter. In fact, her late-stage diagnosis was typical of how medical institutions catering to whites dismissed women of color. "They're thick-skinned." Imagine if we tried to quantify the effect that racial bias in healthcare has had on our well-being.

I'm still trying to deconstruct connections between her mental and physical health and the types of therapeutic options we might be discussing, if incisions and ice pick procedures had not made way for acid and fungi. These had not receded into less invasive cognitive-behavioral approaches.

•••

Eventually, time and some newly acquired knowledge helped me accept with modest objectivity the fact that my mother had been managing, as best she could, her tremendous struggles. The internet became my ally in this endeavor, as there was nothing a search engine could not find. The door was open, and the knowledge was mine, and I realized I would not have had either if it were not for all the quirky opportunities that led me to engage with a world of information through technology.

I learned behavioral disorders and mental illness seldom ride alone; OCD might come with ADHD, and a narcissistic or borderline personality disorder might come with depression. And as I was able to place some perspective on her behaviors and addictions, I understood she most likely had been dealing with one or more issues from her earliest days.

•••

I was almost twenty when I graduated from observing my mother's outbursts with curiosity to igniting them. I would become a foil in the passive-aggressive war she waged against us. I had developed a taste for her salty tête-à-têtes and sour rebukes.

"You are not at all a lady," and "You're not the child I raised," are things I would take from her without revealing how much they felt like compliments.

So, my mother, Dad, and I became an example of dysfunctional functioning quite well. Each of us took a role in our tenuous family relationship, and, like Jenga, you might pull one out to see if it all falls apart.

And then my dad died.

• • •

I was over forty when I knew enough to understand that the breakdown she had after my birth was postpartum psychosis. This condition presents broadly from depression to mood swings, agitation, paranoia, and, in her case, screaming. In retrospect, my mother's postpartum was almost predictable. She had fibroid tumors throughout a complicated pregnancy with perinatal menses. She would recall the doctor presenting my dad with mortal decisions across her gurney as they rushed her into the OR. And she would awaken from a C-section and a radical hysterectomy with other mitigations aggregated into a pregnancy and delivery that would be her first and her last.

• • •

Gynecology has thankfully moved forward since the early '60s, despite the ignorance and politics that have tried to hold it back. Change is slow. But with medicine conceding that female organs are integral to more than reproduction, it is progress. Ignoring the physiologic and often psychogenic consequences of surgeries that once cut wholesale into the female gut to harvest ovaries, fallopian tubes, uterus, infant, et al., is bad medicine; to reduce the anatomical complexities of women to simple biologics is now astigmatic.

My mother might want to tell herself a reassuring story of a pregnancy that came to term despite the odds, and a delivery she believed was sacrosanct. Still, she was under anesthesia, and the limitations of that time left her without a uterus and the hope of a reproductive future. She is still anesthetized in a sense, as she cannot articulate this as another instance of a Black woman encountering her lack of reproductive agency. Black babies are facing mortality. Black bodies account for the decades of progress in women's health that have brought us to where we are today.

• • •

Years passed, and the chasm between my mother and me grew wider. And when I decided to marry, she would let it grow between herself and my spouse and the two children he and I would bring into this world, until the chasm grew to the extent no one knew how to fill it.

And then I got a call.

"We're calling because we received a Life-Alert notification from the San Jose address...emergency vehicles are there now, and the paramedics are tending to Mrs. Hall. Would that be your mother?"

I didn't immediately answer. My heart was in my throat, and it almost made me choke. The caller continued.

"She's ok, ma'am. I mean, she's not injured or anything. Nothing broken."

I would arrive to see the first responders putting their equipment back on the truck. One of them, looking vaguely familiar, would mention that he had answered a call at this address a couple of years ago.

"But we get a lot of calls." He would say with a shrug, avoiding solecisms that might single out my mother.

"But you don't get a lot of these calls." I delivered this as a statement, but it was a question, and rhetorical at that. I could see him searching his thoughts for calls from other seniors, folks who needed nothing more than the type of attention flashing lights and urgency might bring, but his eyes said otherwise. They were apologetic. It was just this senior.

*Yeah*, I thought. Even if this guy would never say a thing like that outright. Yeah.

He didn't have to say it because it was on his face.

And despite this, I struggled to attribute my mother's entanglements to alcohol. I wanted it to be something like bipolar disorder, manic depression, or paranoia, something that, in my limited understanding of mental illness, felt less like a choice.

# Slumber

by Stephani Maari Booker

My therapist said I should sleep with sound,
but no words, no voices. Symphonies, jazz,
even white noise buzz. Just no speech allowed.
I'd been downloading freebie ambiance:
atmospheric tweaks, gurgling creeks, plus
night forest rustles and ocean shore crashes,
singing bowl echoes, tongue drum vibrations —
whispering nature and sonorous metal.

But I prefer to be cradled by storms.
Spending the night on pillows of thunder,
blankets of droplets on roofs, stones, puddles,
leaves, wrapped by sheets of howling wind.
Stilling tinnitus in my ears and the
torment in my head— rain, my comforter.

# Strangulation Necklace

by Monique Reneé Harris

My disabled son is like a necklace around my disabled neck. Each bead is a medical challenge we had to go through: difficult birth to a disabled mother, open heart surgery, autism, blocked ears, seizures, diabetes, COVID, and stroke. Collectively, the necklace of medical traumas makes my dreams go darker and choke me like the spiked iron collars the enslaved used to wear.

**First bead:** In October 1989, my baby had a difficult birth because I have spastic cerebral palsy. Doctors **induced labor**, but because of my disability, they could not give me pain medications, and I refused the epidural because I didn't want to risk paralysis. At eight o'clock the next morning, the doctors held my legs open because when I get nervous, I stiffen up. My attendant helped me push out a five-pound and nine-ounce baby. This struggle to be born was the first bead on the string of his life.

**Second bead:** At a year and a half, we went to San Francisco Hospital for open heart surgery. My son was born with **a hole in his heart**. They had to crack open his chest and put a patch to close the hole. Then they told me he needed a blood transfusion. Fortunately, he and his father have the same blood type. My son spent two weeks in the hospital.

**Third bead**: They tested my baby, and he wasn't hitting the same developmental markers as other babies his age. I said, "He's going to be alright," but he wasn't. He was diagnosed with a learning disability —**Autism**.

**Fourth bead**: I hate doctors. I was traumatized when I was young. My grandmother went to the hospital and never came back. So, each visit to the doctor strikes trauma. My son was growing and doing well for years, but they discovered his **ears were blocked.** We had to go to a children's hospital for an ear operation. I left my baby twice with the doctors. When I left my son, I said, "I hope he comes back to me."

**Fifth bead**: One day, my son was lying in the middle of my bed, and he started shaking. I said, "Brandon. Brandon." No response. I took him to the hospital. The doctor said, "Let's do an MRI." That's when you get inside a big tube to look at your whole body. My son was terrified, but my attendant calmed him down because she was like his grandma to him. They put him in the tube and saw abnormal activity in his brain. He has **seizures.** The doctors prescribed medicine.

**Sixth bead**: My son kept passing out when he had seizures. When they tested his blood, they found his sugar was awfully high, and he had **diabetes**. When they gave him medication, they had to make sure it did not have adverse reactions with his seizure medicines. The old medication caused weight gain, while the new medicines cause weight loss.

**Seventh bead**: My son got COVID. Even worse, my son, whose **kidney disease** requires him to receive a more expensive alternative to Paxlovid, was denied that medicine. This meant that he had to go through COVID without medication. I think COVID put a strain on his kidneys.

**Eighth bead**: **My son had a stroke!** He spent two weeks in the hospital. He got out of the ICU, then entered an excellent rehab for another four weeks. I went back and forth from work to the hospital and rehab to visit him. Slowly, he got better. The last thing he said before they discharged him was, "I don't want to be in a wheelchair like Mama or walk with a cane like Dad."

My disabled son is like a necklace around my disabled neck. I wish I could tear the beads of his medical traumas and throw them away from me, but I can't; they have been a part of who we are since his birth, and *I love him so much*. Love is the clasp.

# Dive into Silence

by Keisha-Gaye Anderson

A mind of shards
spinning
collapsing
crashing
forgetting the combination
to wholeness.

The blinkered lights
of a digital maze
munching on the minutes
and tomorrow's daze
looks just like all the rest
falling away in fast motion.

Bits of people's lives
in pixels
digital quicksand
a time suck
a broken compass, spinning in the infinite scroll.

Which way do our minds go?
Can we even hear ourselves, gather the fragments
of memory to tell a new story?

The noise of wired life is lonesome,
lights so loud and numbing,
a body blinder
oblivious to bombs dropping,
plastic food up-priced,
and ogre men trying to manage wombs.

Let us dive into silence

and wake up
walk straight
through the gate
back to ourselves.

# Mind/Body Wisdom: Discussion Questions

Use these questions to spark conversation about the poems, stories, and essays in this section.

## Acolytes

by Ellen June Wright

1. According to Merriam-Webster, an acolyte is someone who assists a member of the clergy in a liturgical service by performing minor duties. It is also someone who is a disciple, pupil, fan, or devotee. Does the title Acolyte aptly describe our relationship with phones?

2. According to a study by Harmony Healthcare, as of 2025, 47% of phone addicts use the phone to boost their moods. 72% of Gen Z (ages 13-28) think their mental health would improve if apps were less addictive. More than half of Americans want to cut down on phone usage. If this is true, we are allowing phone and app companies to create the brain disease of addiction for future generations. How might we be considered acolytes in this process, and what can we do to reverse this trend and reduce phone dependency?

---

## Organs to the System: Lessons from Fibroid Removal Surgery

by by Violeta Antone

1. In this narrative poem, the speaker tells us she had an operation and had the doctor's orders, but finds it difficult to rest. She keeps forgetting to limit how much she lifts and how far she walks. Her recurring question is, when do we get to practice resting to heal? What are some of the ways you "practice" resting and putting limits on time and energy commitments?

2. The narrative then opens to examine our country as a whole. The poet notes trends in devaluing things like USAID and Medicaid that provide healthcare to those who may not be able to afford it. How does this tie in with rest, and how do you think this impacts a person's mental health?

3. While the focus is on the Black church and Christianity, there are many religions where faith and mental health have integral roles. Think about other religions and their relationship with mental health. Are they similar or different from Christianity?

## She Lives Always Seeking the Silver Lining: Mental Health Challenges and Triumphs Living with Sickle Cell Disease

by Sheila Louise Bennett Marchbanks, aka She-She

1. What did you learn about SCD that you may not have known before?

2. For Sickle Cell Warriors, there are at least three challenges that tie the disease to mental health. What are those three challenges, and what commentary does the author make regarding those challenges?

---

## Mode of Support

by Alora Young

1. In this photo, a person appears to be leaning up against a giant bottle of medicine that is supporting her physically, in an open hallway. Why is the bottle of medicine so large? Do you wonder why the person is in a hallway? What message do you think the photo is conveying?

---

## The Five Stages

by Dr. Ahliah Sharp

1. What did you learn about "second-hand grief"?

2. The author describes how she managed her emotions in the different stages. Was there a response that the author had that surprised you?

3. Reflecting on your own life, was there a time when you were concerned about the health of a loved one, where you could see how you went through the five stages?

4. It is important to honor our experiences. How can we honor our emotions in such a crisis?

---

## Diagnosing It
by Carmen Estela Kennedy Saleh

1. What do you think the father should have or could have done to help protect his daughter from the symptoms of his wife's mental illness?

2. In what ways was the daughter a victim of the mother's illness?

3. What coping strategies did the mother use? Are the doctors at fault in the way they prescribed medication and treated her symptoms? Do you think the mother could have received appropriate medical help?

---

## Slumber
by Stephanie Maari Booker

1. The poet's therapist suggests what she should listen in order to help her fall asleep. However, the poet describes what comforts her and how it "soothes the torment in my head." What do you think her preference suggests about her mindset and health?

2. How would you describe your sleep plans and rituals? What do you think it reveals about you?

---

## Strangulation Necklace
by Monique Harris

1. In this narrative, the narrator walks the reader through some extremely traumatic, physically and emotionally painful experiences. For each experience, there are wonderful celebrations, medical ingenuity, and medicines to help with symptoms, which are just two of the positive provisions that have impacted quality of life. Can you think of any other things?

2. After listing the eight "trauma beads" that create the traumatic life journey of the poet's son, what are some things you think they might be able to do to start unpacking the trauma, healing from the past, and resting in a more sustainable, less traumatic present?

## Dive into Silence
by Keisha-Gaye Anderson

1. *"Sean Parker, one of the early leaders of Facebook, admitted in a 2017 interview that the goal of Facebook's and Instagram's founders was to create "a social-validation feedback loop . . . exactly the kind of thing that a hacker like myself would come up with, because you're exploiting a vulnerability in human psychology." – Jonathan Haidt, The Anxious Generation: How the Great Rewiring of Childhood Caused an Epidemic of Mental Illness*
The poem, coupled with Haidt's quote, is a mental health clarion call for everyone to step away from technology and reconnect in real life. What are some things we can do to turn the tide we are currently surfing?

# Living in Black Skin

Post Traumatic Slave Syndrome is a condition that exists
as a consequence of multigenerational oppression
of Africans and their descendants
resulting from centuries of chattel slavery.
A form of slavery that was predicated on the belief
that African Americans were inherently/genetically
inferior to whites. This was then followed
by institutionalized racism,
which continues to perpetuate injury.

—Dr. Joy DeGruy

# The Mental Health of Slaves

by Kache' Attyana Mumford

*Every generation has mental illness.*
*It lives in the smoke rings that match the silver of a freshly cleaned kitchen sink.*
*The smell lingers in the air long after the ash has disappeared, and people pretend not to cough up their disgust from smelling something burning.*
*The crows, who were simply flying, are berated in the daylight for the deforestation that's not their creation.*
*While accusing, eyes fail to realize that the culprit can be found by wiping the fog off their mirror.*

The first thing I learned while getting my Master's Degree in Therapy was that runaway slaves were listed as being mentally unstable by a licensed psychiatrist. The diagnosis was drapetomania, published in 1851. A disease that causes slaves to run away. A disease-causing rascality, even in black folks who are already free. Samuel A. Cartwright created a name and used scripture to find purity in the vitality of a race he said shouldn't be treated fairly. Just fair enough for no scars to be seen.

*Every slave has a life that should have been free.*
*Every woman deserves to raise her babies.*
*To snatch her heart after it was pushed out of her chest*
*And running before the blood set would send every living creature into madness.*

The second thing I learned while getting my master's degree in Therapy was that I would be trapped in a classroom with only one other person who looked like me. Forced to carry the weight of answers to my history when my one ally left me. We started the degree with six black women, and now there is just me. As I repeat, "runaway slaves were projected to have a mental disease," balancing between the explanation of why the "N"- word harms people like me.

*Madness:*
*Being stripped, sold, owned with a life*
*that should have been yours to hold.*

Madness:
Being the only black person in the class.
Being the only one who knows-
She wasn't meant to exist.

# Acceptance Letter: Welcome, poet, to Graduate Studies

by Jordan E. Franklin

Another degree in and you know nothing from nothing.
If you want a live staging of Ginsberg's "Howl," head
to the bus depot. If you want to see a dying riverbed, look
in the veins of the "actors" that sleep there. Be sure to catch
all those nights Main Street lights up, making the Bed-Stuy's
of your youth jealous, yet still, the closest you've been to
an unfriendly gun has been on the good side of a schoolyard
fence or ducking windowsills on Pacific St. at New Year's.
For fun, take comprehensive exams like Xanax, dream
of insurance good enough for a therapist or a support dog.
One peer recommends magnets. Another, a good showerhead
and weed, but you know you need these cracks in your brain
to write. In Her office, amongst Her books,
Professor says, *you don't look like a poet, but you'll do.*

# Depression: Black & Female

by Kache' Attyana Mumford

There's one quote I love to sing,
plucked low from a stuttering guitar—
a blues so heavy and lonesome
it cracks open the pain of ancestors,

*People always stop right before*
*they get what they've worked for.*

I am not giving up.

I'm buried beneath a mountain of peach sheets,
not a fraction of me moving—
except for the slight cave of my stomach,
the opposing rise of my chest—
proof I'm still breathing.

Eyes closed, but not sleeping.
Every time I do,
nightmares strangle me
I gasp awake, only to find
more enemies waiting in reality.

My head pounds with a migraine
pulsing down my spine—

But this not giving up.
is more than just failing.
My nose is buried in freshly washed cotton;
skin smells of cocoa butter and vanilla mist.
If I had a job,
I'd rise,
let my ego fall to the floor,
paint on a smile that pinches the corners of my mouth
and live out the day
until my weary bones come to rest
on those same freshly washed sheets.

Across the room:
a basket of clean laundry.
I'm not folding.

*People always stop right before*
*they get what they've worked for.*

I am not giving up.

I'm willing my body not to cry—
My fist clenches, unclenches,
to quiet the fear
that makes my right handshake.

My thoughts loop:
how much I want a drink—
Haitian rum, a margarita,
cheap wine,
anything over ten percent.

But I'm not drinking.
Not since I quit cold turkey—
*to prove I'm more than the thing I do*
when I'm lonely, sad, and struggling.

In the past twelve days,
I've read eleven books.
Almost one a day:
two poetry,
one self-help,
two nonfiction,
a book on war,
countless romance,
and one about faith.

But really, they're all about faith.
I am not giving up.
And I'm not just failing.
As I write this, I'm holding my breath—
forcing my body to take breaks
every 3 minutes and 16 seconds.

Yesterday was Mother's Day.
I wrote a card that made her call me
her *little wordsmith*,
a name that bathes me in honey
as sweet as her Southern charm.

Today, I've ignored my mother's calls twice

when I hear wordsmith,
my mind autocorrects to work less,
which becomes worthless.

My mother and sister are texting
about how she needs to give away her dog;
and even though I'm his favorite person,
I can't help.
I'm twenty-seven, back in the bed I had at seventeen
the one I swore I'd never need again
once I blew out the candles at nineteen.

But the world is burning.
Grants for the arts are drying up.
We are losing empathy.

I couldn't even leave a theatre in West Virginia
without being called a slur.
Co-workers rushed to explain
*how slavery was humane*
*...at least they were given room and board.*
They expected me to nod.

I am not giving up.
I'm more than failing.

Because in the next ten seconds,
I'll get out of bed—
make coffee
clean everything until it shines
and reflects the dis-ease
no one else can see.

I'll work out until my muscles scream,
and apply, apply, apply.

...one quote I love to sing,
plucked low from a stuttering guitar—

*People always stop right before*
*they get what they've worked for.*

# Racism & Post-Traumatic Stress Disorder (PTSD)

**What is Racial Trauma?**
People can experience racial trauma from something that happens directly to them or from seeing others mistreated because of their race. Coverage of events caused by racial discrimination in the media can also be upsetting, and repeated viewing or frequent media accounts can amplify those feelings.

**Impact of Racial Trauma**
Racial trauma can lead to an increased risk of physical and mental health problems, emotional difficulties, such as stress, anxiety, depression or PTSD. After experiencing racial discrimination, people may have unwanted memories and may avoid thoughts, feelings and reminders of racial trauma. People may feel on guard and on high alert, and have trouble with concentration, sleep or irritability.

**Coping with Racial Trauma**

- **Empowerment strategies.** Some people may find advocacy for reducing discrimination or oppression meaningful.
- **Values-based goal setting.** Identifying specific goals that align with personal values (e.g. family, community, equity, self-improvement, security) can be another way to feel more in control and enjoy life.
- **Self-care and lifestyle changes.** Taking time to recuperate from racial trauma on a regular basis is important. Taking walks, listening to music or relaxation techniques may help.
- **Taking charge of emotions.** Relaxation and mindfulness strategies can be helpful in countering the effects of stress on the body and mind.
- **Social support.** Talking to supportive people about thoughts and feelings related to racial trauma can be validating.
- **Media balance:** Limit exposure to "doomscrolling," or focusing on negative and discouraging media content.
- If self-care is not enough to cope with the impact of racial trauma in daily life, seeking professional help can be valuable.

Source: U.S. Dept. of Veterans Affairs. PTSD: National Center for PTSD. (2025, March 26). Retrieved April 26, 2026. https://www.ptsd.va.gov/understand/types/racial_trauma.asp

# Sticky Notes.

Artist: Davian Chester

Today is a great day because you are here
You are APPRECIATED!
Stay Positive!
You are stronger than you think.
Hello Beautiful
Know your WORTH!
2023

# Curing Eldest Daughter Disease

by Tiara Jones

**Diagnosis:** Eldest Daughters Disease
**Case Notes:** African American, eldest of 4, Virgo mother with possible personality disorder, recent ADHD diagnosis, raised conservative Christian (i.e., anti-EVERYTHING), purity messaging, good girl programming, self-sacrificing for the greater good.
**Severity?** Really, Really Bad

Basically, I was born screwed up, but you wouldn't know that by looking at me. My shiny eldest daughter's exterior is coated in graduating from a ritzy boarding school, amassing two shiny degrees and two braggable certifications, marked by a well-stamped passport, a sexy six-figure salary, and disposable income complete with multiple investment accounts. From the outside, I look successful, but I have never ever once felt it. Growing up, I was historically the smart Black girl who routinely presented all A's with little effort. I hated reading and studied for spelling tests the night before, and school just came easily. That was... until I transferred to a fancy college prep school. My identity shifted as I left my safe, small, private Black middle-class Christian school and stepped into the big leagues of privileged white supremacy, I mean, Cranbrook Educational Community.

Like most Black parents, my mom gave me "the talk" ... you know THE TALK. Not the birds and the bees, but the "You're Black, so you're basically a second-class citizen" talk. I know Black parents mean well, telling us things like, "We have to work twice as hard to get half as far." Still, it can create an inferiority complex, especially when coming from the people you love the most. To constantly associate whiteness with what is "better" insinuates that Blackness is not as good. Moving into a wealthy white environment, I instantly felt less than everyone around me. She might as well have sent me into a shark tank on my menstrual cycle. I felt like I was on the front lines of an excavation into how the other half lives, and I felt the bumps from the very first day. At my previous private school, we paid a book fee, and our books were presented on the first day of school. Here, everyone ordered them themselves, and I didn't have books for a good two weeks. I went into the bathroom that first day, put my feet on the seat, and cried.

The transition was so hard for me. I had never switched classes before and immediately struggled with the heavier workload and increased need for organization. School has always come easily, and I never had to try previously. At my new school, everything felt hard, and it felt like everyone expected me to figure out how to get by on my own. I was losing my identity; if I wasn't the smart girl, who was I? The poor Black girl from Detroit? I tried my best to fit in and somehow wound up being bullied... by two Black girls at that. Little did they know, I was more afraid of my mama than them, so they could take their little peer pressure somewhere else. Their bullying initiated my therapy journey in 7th grade. I had to choose between a white woman therapist and a Black man who was my friend's stepdad. I chose my friend's dad, but I figured I wouldn't tell him too much of my business, so I wouldn't be dinner table fodder. Damn trusting patient client confidentiality, I couldn't trust it.

I spent a good 10-15 years in therapy only to realize my parents were the problem, well, not exactly, but that's basically what the book *Adult Children of Emotionally Immature Parents* said. I realized my family constructed the eldest daughter role for me, and I somehow adopted it.

**Role Self - Eldest Daughter Programming Formula:**

> *Great example, no needs, all knowing, all giving, self-forsaking, high performing, rule follower (at least externally), charismatic, always says the right thing, peacekeeper with no feelings (unless it's that time of the month, then she's fussing), puts everyone before herself, taught she belonged last, taught to be good, be humble, be devoted, and be a long-suffering, noncritical thinking Christian servant.*

**Programming Successfully Adopted.**

I carried the mantle of being a "good example" to children both within and outside my household, and I still bear the remnants of that pressure to this day. It wasn't until this year that I realized this "Perfect Eldest Daughter" bubble is really a prison that keeps me isolated and alone. Perfection has always separated me from the "regular people," even though, with a recent ADHD diagnosis in hand, I've been considered lazy at times. I was taught to follow the script that makes everyone else happy. I was conditioned to deny myself in life and love. I was perpetually juggling between being a fixer and a people pleaser, adding whatever value I could to prove myself worthy of being needed. I built so many relationships based on trauma bonds that eroded away like sand over the years. I didn't know how to coexist healthily with myself or others.

I feel like my unhealthy relationships began with my mom. Through therapy, I realized our relationship was more of an enmeshment than anything. As her child, I was her best friend, but I am not sure she was mine. She was the sun, and I was the moon, a reflection of her, her chance to right the wrongs of her childhood. She tried to live through me. She tried to control me under the guise of "wanting what was best for me." She planted seeds of doubt that made it hard for me to trust myself. Her voice was often louder in my head than my own. My friendships mirrored hers, collecting "broken people" who "needed" me. She killed my artist dreams by condemning art school and saying my parents would never pay for that. She twisted the knife by saying, "They're called starving artists for a reason, and she didn't think I could starve that well."

So I didn't go to an art school; I went to a racist Christian College instead, which further alienated me. Unexpectedly followed by transferring to my HBCU, Fisk University, which baptized me in Black waters and renewed my sense of self. Gifted me the gift of individuality. At Fisk, I was just me, not the delegate for the whole Black race. I spent a beautiful three years wrapped in an ebony cocoon, which harshly ejected me back into the white world that immediately tried to humble me and succeeded.

The world became so scary to me. As a confident Black woman unprotected, I was told loudly that there was no place for me. Corporate America attempted to ensure my mental unravelling. Mind games were never my forte, and these white people had decades of experience navigating these halls, which were not made for me. They ran circles around me, while I shrank to stay safe. I became scared of being seen. Trauma colored the lens through which I saw the world.

Everywhere I looked, I saw red; I saw danger. The future I used to cling to for hope became a place of perpetual fear. All I could think about was navigating the next hardship. Surviving to fight another day, proving that I was capable and that I belonged. Anxiety ruled my body, as butterflies took up permanent residence in my stomach and chest. My nervous system was perpetually activated, living through trauma after trauma. I did not know peace.

A complex person loves a complex solution. I remember first hearing about the power of meditation, journaling, gratitude, prayer, moving your body, etc. I disregarded it and thought it was too easy, too hippy dippy. I was sure I needed to take more challenging actions to get more hardcore results. I did not understand how these little things could have such a big impact until I learned more about neuroplasticity and the brain's ability to rewire itself. I discovered more about my attachment style and my mother-wound, and realized the love, nurturing, protection, and guidance I had been looking for could be provided by a healthier, better-resourced me.

Over the years in therapy, I've been building my emotional toolkit and watering myself. I have been calling my energy back in and reinvesting my focus into myself. I am loving from a place of wellness and not desperation. I am centering myself. I am saving myself. I am shedding a life that appears successful. I am rejecting the role-self, rediscovering my true self, and curing my eldest daughter's disease by coming home to me.

I have been waiting for me, and I welcome myself with open arms.

# Scars

by Dana I. Hunter

Follow the lines
connect the dots
my razor is kind
with the images it wrought.

Can your fingertips read
the braille on my body?
Bumps into letters,
letters into sentences,
birth stories unmentionable.

This skin has a tale to tell
I see them for what they are
witnesses to the pain I hide
mirrored events journaled into flesh.

# Sonya

by Beverly Head

Perhaps she had her own evil spirits
To battle,
But in front of her house
She looked like an angel
In her long white robe.
The two cops claimed that they were there to help.
She tried to explain to them about prowlers, her broken car windows.
They asked for her ID, came into her home.
As she searched through her clutter of papers,
She had an inkling that something was not right.
She asked for a Bible.
The big one told her to dump her steaming hot water
From the pot that was on the stove.
When she turned from the stove with the pot of hot water
In her hands and looked into his face,
She realized that she had allowed a demon into her home.
She tried to rebuke him in the name of Jesus,
But it was too late.
Angry that his true face had been revealed,
The demon swore, yelled that he would shoot her
In her fucking face.
He drew his gun.
She said that she was sorry.
He shot Sonya in her head.
The demon declared, she's done.

*Sonya Massey, a 36-year-old unarmed Black woman, was murdered by Sean Grayson, a 30-year-old deputy in Woodside Township near Springfield, Illinois, on July 6, 2024. He was found guilty on Jan. 29, 2026. He is now serving a 20-year sentence.

# Love, Joy, Peace, Patience, Kindness, Goodness, Faithfulness

by Ginger M. Galloway

phone call to interrupt
the interrogation
of me
or you
or him
do I know who you are?
do I recognize your voice?
I will not lie
because truth is all that we have
looking for convincing words
I don't like him

*shut up*

take that glass away
no water
no
I am not afraid of what might happen
I am afraid of
training
and black and white vehicles
if we just don't call black and white vehicles
white faces
red and blue lights shining into the windows

We just want to know that she is safe

*She is safe*

I am not afraid
for me
I am afraid
of people unseen
and the tape on rewind
playing backwards
singing the fruit of the spirit
in the parking lot
love, joy, peace, patience,
kindness, goodness, faithfulness

*shut up*

holding back tears
i can't let him see

that I am looking for you
when will they come
with little pills that you can see
vials of blood
Certainly, this must be drug-induced
without the words drug induced
because mostly they are

***drug induced***
***isn't that what you think?***
***words you say with your eyes.***

but they don't come with results
only water in Styrofoam cups
they don't come in white coats or
dress slacks
they don't come
except for urine
and more water
and sandwiches on white bread
mayonnaise in foil packets
i am not afraid

*sit down*

they send security to watch
curtains open

*sit down*

sharp movements

*shut up*

the fruit of the spirit's not a coconut

*the fruit*
*the*
*the*
*the the*
*the fruit*

the fruit of the spirit's not a coconut
if you want to be a coconut, you might as well hear it

*just run*
*to Harriet Tubman*
*or like Harriet*

like a runaway slave?
I laugh
we will laugh
one day we will laugh
we must laugh
when you are safe
and they are gone
eating fruit from your garden
tea with honey

Bible study and poems
Of you
I'm not

*afraid*

I won't apologize
for love
just don't be gone

# The Pretending Game

by Tiffany Smalls

Stop building bridges over bodies,
deal with what's been left at your feet.

The honesty of death
shakes your faith,

you must think these thoughts
never cross my mind.

We cannot heal
if we can't acknowledge the wound.

I want to talk
about how it hurts to be alive,

how I have never been able
to unshoulder this burden.

Superlatives caption me:
"Most likely to wear a noose as a necklace."

There must be a secret lineage of
quiet decay in our family tree.

Are these roots
nested in the grave?

I may not be strong enough
to see the branches stretch through time,

my bough might snap,
and I might hang

a white flag from twigs.
Surrender this heirloom.

Let the bark rot
and the leaves turn muddy soup,

but if whispers catch breeze,
and blow the truth across landscape —

Oh! How we could grow
and live, a future of flowers blooming,

the fruit ripe,
and still hanging on.

# Turn the Soil

by Keisha-Gaye Anderson

Listen. Before you believe
those acrid whispers funneling up
from the basement of your mind
hissing that you are unloved and unlovable,
a burden and insufferable,
roll your eyes back into time
and look for where the dead body is buried.

Which sapling of you was chopped down
before reaching the sun
because you were too clear of a mirror?

Whose fear became an axe
and hacked you to pieces
before you could fully unfurl?

Our composted selves
release a noxious fog
bending our vision into
funhouse mirrors.

It's time now to turn the soil
into a garden.

# Living in Black Skin: Discussion Questions

Use these questions to spark conversation about the poems, stories, and essays in this section.

## The Mental Health of Slaves

by Kache' Attyana Mumford

1. *We started the degree with six black women, and now there is just me.* Have you ever been in a situation or observed one in which you discerned or experienced something similar? Were you able to identify it at the time and articulate it? How did it make you feel?

2. Before reading this narrative poem, did you know about drapetomania and how Black people were victimized and institutionalized in asylums?

---

## Acceptance Letter: Welcome, poet, to Graduate Studies

by Jordan E. Franklin

1. The speaker in this sonnet makes a literary allusion to *Howl* by Ginsberg. This poem rejects the "classic" concepts of what it means to be an American. Why do you think the speaker references the Beat poet, Ginsberg, and the poem *Howl*?

2. This graduate student is a disenfranchised member of society. How do we know, and what does it matter? Why is the professor so dismissive? What would you do if you were the speaker in this poem?

---

## Depression: Black & Female

by Kache' Attyana Mumford

1. Why does the speaker in this poem say the eleven books she has read from different genres are "all about faith"?

2. There are a few reasons the speaker feels like a failure in this poem. What are they? Why is she angry? What can she control? What are her current and future hopes? How is this impacting her mental health?

3. At the conclusion of the poem, does the speaker sound like she is in a mentally healthy place? She says she plans to apply for jobs and grants. Is she hopeful about either? How do we know? What advice would you give the speaker?

---

## Sticky Notes

by Davian Chester

1. The person in the image is crying and looking into a mirror with several sticky notes bearing positive affirmations. What do you think the artist is conveying? Why is the person crying? Are positive affirmations effective in helping people in their mental health journey, or is it just a nice idea? Discuss your reason for your response.

---

## Curing Eldest Daughter Disease

by Tiara Jones

1. The first complaint the daughter has is with "the talk" her parents gave her. Do you think they are right? What is her concern regarding what she is told?

2. What does the daughter's experience in different schools indicate? She labels schools racist or supportive, but doesn't tell us how. Do you think solid examples are important, or does what she tells us sound plausible enough? Why/why not?

3. What does the eldest daughter decide to do to guide her towards healing, and what role does she decide to take on?

---

## Scars
by Dana I. Hunter

1. What are the scars, and how does this poem work on two different levels?

---

## Sonya
by Beverly Head

1. Do you know what procedures police should follow if they are dealing with someone who has symptoms of a mental illness?

2. What protocol do you think should be followed?

---

## Love, Joy, Peace, Patience, Kindness, Goodness, Faithfulness
by Ginger M. Galloway

1. *Scientists can say with confidence that racism is bad for Black mental health.* – Rheeda Walker. What is the poet's main concern in the poem?

# Abuse and Resilience

As long as you keep secrets and suppress information,
you are fundamentally at war with yourself...
The critical issue is allowing yourself
to know what you know.
That takes an enormous amount of courage.

– Bessel A. van der Kolk

# Funny, In Hindsight

by Quan Williams

Alright, so this is a true story in my world of navigating mental health issues in my Black family. I have a more humorous perspective. This is in no way meant to minimize the severity of the topic. Poor mental health has had a devastating impact on me and some people I know. I just want to honor Black people's long tradition and expertise in making lemonade out of lemons.

My mom's lack of mental wellness isn't funny at all, but in hindsight, the way I dealt with certain situations is funny. What I was thinking during the time it happened is funny. You see, my mother was diagnosed with several serious mental health disabilities. As a kid, I did not know there was a diagnosis for what she was dealing with. I just knew that she was on a frequency of her own, and that she would often switch up her channels suddenly and without much warning. She had a habit of thinking that I was looking at her funny - funny, as in a disrespectful way. Most of the time, I literally had no clue what she was talking about.

This particular time, I was in a zone listening to *Another Bad Creation* on the radio. I had the biggest crush on Red, and his part was coming up when she asked why I was looking at her like "That," meaning disrespectfully. This was my immediate cue that things were about to get violent. I didn't even know she was in the room, so I certainly was not looking at her in any particular kind of way. I stood up so that running would be an option. My favorite hobby was playing football outside with the boys, and I figured maybe a Walter Payton move was in my playbook if I needed it. Before I could ask anything or reply, she threw one of my sister's plastic baby bottles at me. The bottle had milk in it, so it flew past me with force. I was an oversized kid, and am still an oversized adult, but I felt a little athletic for being able to dodge that one. My sweet moves escaped me quickly because her next throw was a glass baby bottle that hit me in the face. So much for thinking I would be the first girl to play for the Chicago Bears. I had been juking the fellas on the football field! However, when elusiveness mattered most, I could not figure out how to get out of the way.

I don't remember what lie I told teachers and classmates about why I had a black eye. This was most likely because that episode was just one in a constant series of violence that I experienced and witnessed growing up in an unhealthy household.

Fast forward thirty-five years, and my mother is sober. She ditched the alcohol and drugs that exacerbated her mental health issues, and she got into talk therapy. She takes prescribed medication, and she has been studying to be a drug and alcohol recovery counselor. To top that off, she's a successful grandmother and one of the dopest people I know - no pun intended. I am really thankful that we both survived some of the worst times, and we now get to grow together and create good times.

Therapy has a lot to do with our ability to coexist harmoniously. I have been in therapy for a long time and definitely believe God used it to save my life. That's how I know the gift of a good God-ordained therapist. Part of my own healing journey was introducing my mother to the idea of going to therapy. I shared with her a joke I had heard: many people are in therapy because of family members who refuse to go. Not one to be the butt of jokes or looked at strangely, my mother eventually called the number I gave her, and she has been in therapy ever since.

Sometimes things still get wicked between my mother and me - especially when her sick expressed thoughts trigger mine. Despite the ill times that still occasionally happen, I am always going to search for the best balance that I can physically and mentally have. There are moments when that balance feels far off. Nevertheless, I am committed to the therapeutic process. I am here today because of the wonders God can do through divine counsel. And even at my grown age, I keep a football with me for the times I am like my mother and want to throw something. Of course, I make sure that the person I'm throwing the football to knows it's coming and enjoys playing catch.

# Father's Death

by George Hammons

(A Blessing)

*Some people are just mean*
*they have something inside them that doesn't understand kindness*
*they take it as a sign of weakness or stupidity and they can't ignore it*
*they have to try to rule over it or crush it.*

As Aunt Ruth spoke those words
The old man in the coffin behind her
seems to smile in agreement

He was just mean

When he was seventeen
he killed his little brother
a hunting accident
but everyone suspected

He was just mean

Two years later
he was court-martialed from the army
something to do with the death of a sergeant
but no one could prove anything
so, the court-martial and dishonorable discharge had to do

He was just mean

He once held a gun to my mother's head
and pulled the trigger

but something went wrong
and the gun didn't fire

He
being insane
got angry at the guy
who had sold him the gun
so, he rushed out
looking for his money back

My mother being terrified
gathered everything she could carry
(except her kids)
and caught the first bus out of town

Aunt Ruth has come to the conclusion
That there won't be a eulogy
*If you can't say something nice... You know.*

# Home

by George Hammons

I think about our disjointed
almost acrobatic childhood
and one night in particular

the four of us poised
upon a rickety wooden bench
huddled like baby birds

Me reaching down in the dark
to pluck a few blades of sanity
from the unmowed chaos

Here where I thought nothing could hurt me
but now we sit hair's breadth whispering
into a calamity

our voices become small like flecks in stone
or weary like rust
only to fade like smoke into the dark

2:30 A.M.
and us with school in the morning
I'm 7 and sleepless

something frightening is in our house
like a pacing tiger or a time bomb
or a ghost

and just like that
our youth is devoured
in angry intoxicated gulps

we will never know the truth of it
except that it has left us unable
to embrace one another

as if to do so would awaken
what it is we have so astutely
learned to fear

# On the Bus

by George Hammons

I am riding the bus.
        *i want to get away from myself,*
but whenever the bus stops
        *i can't get off,*
I have to keep riding.
        after a while i feel so warm
I have to take off my coat.
        *suddenly, it becomes a cape.*
        *and i fear i am too exposed*
        *because i don't have a mask*
so, I tear off one of my coat's sleeves
and cut eye holes with my pocketknife.
a lady sitting across from me
        *who looks exactly like my little sister*
quietly asks, "Honey are you ok?"
I tell her,
        "I will be, as soon as I put on my mask."

# Moonslick

by Eric DeVaughnn

some boys are taught to tremble
to temper their boil and burn
through stippled scars—and best
not look like the trauma they are.

mommas lather sons in grease
and shine; given to this ritual hunt
for all the ways to reflect a daylight
we only know how to dim.

# The Wound I Won't Stop Touching

by Angelique Zobitz

I wanted love to be a green thing—
a sapling, stubborn and sure,
deep-rooted enough to outlast winter.

Instead, it was always a wildfire,
bright and crackling, beautiful for a moment,
then ash and ember.

I mistook longing for hunger,
hunger for need,
need for something worth keeping.

I wish I were the kind of woman who knows how to quit,
who doesn't set herself on fire just to keep someone warm,
who doesn't mistake a locked door for a shelter,
a mouthful of apologies for a love song.

I've spent a lifetime calling wreckage devotion.
Loving men who loved me like a clenched fist,
like a storm warning, like a road with no return.

Love like a river with no mouth,
only current,
only drag.

Love like the horse that bucks the hardest
before it breaks.

I let love make a ruin of me—
an altar, a burial ground, a mess too sacred to sweep clean.

I have let men brand their names into my body,
swore it was holy, called it fate,
refused to name it the ruin it was.

I wanted love like hunger,
like the ache of a fast gone too long.
A man who would pray me into the red cathedral of his chest,
etch me into the fault lines of his palms,
speak my name in tongues until I came undone.

What is a damaged man but a red flag waving?
I was the girl who mistook suffering for strength,
survival, the same as being loved.

Because of this,
the past is a wound I won't stop touching,
a scar I press, just to make sure it still hurts.

# Drawn to Abusive Men in My Youth

by Jasmine Vallejo-Love

I floated to dysfunction like a barge – slow –
as if there was no ample warning
signs of paranoia and jealousy,
some bright orange depressions bobbing in the sea.

That isla was not bonita,
swamped with broken bones and memories,
the mist of anger and regret like fog,
I couldn't claim to see clearly.

But it was foreshadowed
in rough nights and rude calculations.
A turn left or right would have saved me.
But I was beached in sour connotations,
on that isla of exploitation
steeped in the soil of the soulless.

# You Never Laid a Hand on Me

by Jasmine Vallejo-Love

you didn't have to.
I flinched at the lunges and fake-outs,
acquiesced to the raised fist,
quieted at your yells and growls.

A firm look was enough
to attenuate my resolve,
know I should never say a word
about who I am.

Your misogyny wafted,
like intoxicating perfume
carrying the weighted message –
bury it. Bury it deep.

I dug a seven-foot grave.
Extra for good measure,
lest you try to trick me out
in a drunken rage.

So sure-footed in my deception
that years beyond your house,
lying in the muck you created,
I denied my butterfly wings.

Now frail, your salty words
fall short of stinging
as I worm my way out
into sunshine.

# Corpus Delicti

by Stephanie Liggins

Too many of us, too often
Navigate life through lonely places
Though not alone, our thoughts only visit our own orbit
And are void of concern for others
Too often, too many of us.
When trouble comes, some of us awaken
And see humanity, a living soul
Too often, many of us don't.

Hatha yoga class was sparse, with only a few of our usual delegation of seasoned women.

The lights were dimmed. The music was soft and soothing as we participated in asanas and pranayamas. We sought to gain the unity of body and mind that yoga is meant to achieve. Leaving the stress of life behind, we stretched, inhaled, and exhaled with a sigh as our 70-year-old instructor modeled.

The yoga room was in the rear of the gym, among several other rooms along the back wall. One would need to know its exact location to find it quickly, as there was no sign. Enroute, no less than forty men of all ages- but primarily young- pumped iron, lifted their muscle-bound bodies on the power tower and machines meant to tone and build muscle. They sweated to impress, working hard to build a fortification of skin and bones and muscles strong.

I felt safe in the building with what felt like brawn cops all around and dispersed along the path to the yoga room.

A few minutes into our session, a woman in her mid-30s entered, breaking the old-lady-only attendance rule that day. She wore kindness on her pretty face. She was matronly: a bit overweight, dressed in sweats, hair pulled back by a scrunchie, and carrying her own mats. She smiled at me when our eyes met: an uncommon human connection in this self-absorbed society. I returned her acknowledgment and got back to the task at hand before I missed any more yoga instruction.

Doing downward dog and child's pose and spinal twists.... I felt like a brittle rubber band about to pop. Entranced by movement after movement, an approaching spirit violated my concentration. I heard angry voices growing louder. I turned to look out the room's glass enclosure and saw two men storming toward the yoga room. The doors were closed, but their voices were so loud they penetrated the glass barrier. Surely, the multitude of Mr. Olympians outside heard and saw these boisterous men. Surely, the people at the front desk, with dress shirts, slacks, and Florsheim dress shoes, saw them and attempted to stop them. Surely, someone would notice that danger was approaching and question the environment that had been created. Right? Someone??

Five older women on the floor did not know how to take the warrior pose. The 70-year-old instructor continued to direct when the men charged into the room until the angry, animated profanity began to fly. They approached the young woman violently. Suddenly, everyone was shocked into attention.

The instructor yelled, "You are disrupting my class!"

The expected response was twice as loud: "I don't give a fuck about your class!"

No further opposition was provided. The men marched up to the younger woman. Standing to her feet, her fear was palpable.

Again, our eyes met. For a moment in time, we were the only two people in the universe as I asked her, "Are you okay?"

She replied timidly, "I don't know."

Off my mat, this old lady in socks ran to the front desk and pleaded for the police to be called, for help to be summoned. Please?! Send help!! Be help!! Help?!!!!

By that time, the terrified young woman was being driven out of the gym by these men. Three male managers came out from behind the counter and asked, "What is going on?!" But dress shirts, slacks, and dress shoes are not the clothes of war; thus, their words were not followed by action. All the Mr. Olympians continued to work towards competing for their title in decided oblivion.

If the woman had been white, would the world have stopped to help her?

I scurried away under the false belief that help was to be had. Yet when I looked back, the angry men had forced her outside the building. No one followed. She was defenseless and alone with the wolves growling at her throat.

I felt beaten, defeated, vulnerable, powerless, weak. What could a 60-year-old woman do for a young female stranger accosted by a short, stocky Tasmanian devil of a man and a taller, scowling man who were attempting to arrest this terrified woman without a warrant or reason?

She was every woman—likely a mother, a wife, a sister, a daughter, a friend. Discounted.

There was no help--not even from me, though I tried. I went back to the yoga room with a heart filled with sadness. I needed to get my shoes, my mat, and my things. My time there could not, would not continue. It should not. I noticed that her mat was still there, as if she would return unscathed to use it. Hopeful. The yoga instructor had returned to instructing, and the room of seasoned women had continued in their class as if nothing had interrupted their unconsciousness. No one cared. A young woman had just been forced from among us, and there was no response. Her humanity had been disregarded. The world continued to go around.

I could not stay another second in that gym. At the front desk, I asked what had been done to help the young woman. The three primped managers responded that they had no jurisdiction once the men had taken her outside the establishment. Once outside, one of the men struck her, I was told. That is all they knew. And they returned behind the counter as if all was well with the world.

I cried out, "You witnessed a woman being abused, and you did nothing?! Did you call the police?"

Their facial expressions said no, but one voice said, "Yes." I waited a few minutes at the door to see if the police arrived. I wanted to be a witness. I wanted them to save this woman who was nowhere to be found. She had been hit and then disappeared.

Was she forced into a car? Was she forced into a trunk? Did she matter? Did anything matter? The police did not come. I could no longer concentrate or think about calling them myself. I looked back at those at the front desk.

No blood on the dress shirts. No wrinkles in the slacks. No scuffs on the dress shoes. Perhaps that is the most important thing after all: self-preservation.

Suddenly, I could not breathe. My heart was palpitating. I felt myself shrinking into a ball of dust. I had to get to my car and lock the door before the boogey man got me, and I completely disappeared into its grasp.

That day, a woman may have died tragically and violently. At the same time, the world around her continued doing what they were doing. Why do we build strength for bodies that do not help? Why do we stretch and twist bodies that discount everyone else's bodies? Why do we not know that alone we are nothing? We are one, or we are none. Can someone please write that in the sky so the world can read it?

Too many of us, too often
Navigate life through lonely places
Though not alone, our thoughts only visit our own orbit
And are void of concern for others
Too often, too many of us.
When trouble comes, some of us awaken
And see humanity, a living soul
Too often, many of us don't.

Over 1 in 3 women and 1 in 6 men in the U.S. experience contact sexual violence, physical violence, or stalking by an intimate partner in their lifetime, totaling over 10 million people annually(National Library of Medicine). If you or someone you know is experiencing abuse, help is available. You can contact the National Domestic Violence Hotline (1-800-799-SAFE or text "START" to 88788).

# Black Women's Loneliness Crisis

by Amaya Marshall

As humans, especially as women, we have been wired by patriarchal constraints to center our lives on finding love. Love, a powerful source of communion between minds and bodies, has been warped into a commodity and a method of control. Loneliness is a real fear that's instilled into women since we buy into the lie of romance and sex being our sole value. *Never wear that hairstyle, don't say that, don't be so loud, don't have a mind of your own, a man won't like that.* This brainwashing has stripped women of our identities and dreams under the threat of loneliness.

The black woman knows this old lie all too well. The lie we've been told has been conveyed to us in multiple ways and by different people, some from our own people. This has placed us in a rather complicated situation. Where we long for love but are told we're undeserving of it if we don't fit into the popular image of what a woman is. All while we are being persuaded to date and stay with men who will cause our own demise.

Growing up as a young black girl, my first exposure to romantic love was something unstable and untrustworthy. Arguing was something I grew accustomed to at home. For money, chores, and basic hygiene, it all came from one source: my grandfather. My grandmother has been living with my grandfather, and she continues to live with him to this day. Having previously lived with him when I was little, he could go from having small periods of "love," "love" turned to drunken stupidity and incompetence, and incompetence turned into full episodes of physical abuse.

The first time I witnessed it was when I was eleven. I had come back from my great-grandmother's house, and I was met by my grandfather with a crazed look, as if all emotion had been drained from his face. "I'm gonna kill you!" He shouted at my grandmother before attacking her in her own bedroom.

The second time it happened was a year later; this time, I was inside the house when it began. I heard my grandmother yell at him, terrified, that's when he started beating her again. My mother wanted to get us out as fast as we could, but he kept us from escaping when he had threatened my mother's life in front of me. Being twelve, and witnessing the man who my grandmother had been staying with for years, and silently tolerating his abuse, begin physically assaulting both her and my mother felt indescribable. It was pure outrageousness in my head that she would remain with him after suffering at his hands.

After all these events, they all led to the same thing. My grandmother entered a state of denial about his actions. Trying to sell me a different picture than the one we just saw, a useless one considering that I was the one who had to see my grandfather throw her and my mother on the hard driveway. It wasn't fair for me to have to keep silent about what had happened, like she was. Why would she remain with a man like that?

I still feel anger and hurt for her attempting to rewrite history against my will.

Still, now that I have matured, I unfortunately know that she bought into the lie of loneliness. She believes her life has no value beyond the man she's tied to. Love had been weaponized against her. "Love" as a method of control over her mind. "Love" as a hopeless bid against loneliness.

Black women face a significant risk of domestic violence. This open secret is often ignored intentionally at best or mocked for laughs at worst. As we see black female celebrities face abuse from their partners, most notably the case of Rihanna and Chris Brown, she was made fun of relentlessly, and pseudo-intellectual patriarchs made think pieces on what she did to "deserve it." The man who nearly beat her to death, mutilated her face, continues to have a massive following, is treated like the victim, and she is the one who is to blame and mocked. This culture of victim blaming against women, especially against black women, has placed black women in a state of denial of their own experiences or a sense of unwillingness to speak out.

This anti-victim narrative we live in has caused black women to remain in bad situations. The black household has also enabled this belief system. Keeping all harm "inside the house" and "stay out of grown folks' business" cultivates this cycle. Forcing black women and girls to bottle up their feelings, their very sense of right and wrong, will warp how they interact as they get older. Telling a young black girl not to question why daddy hurts mommy when he comes from work will have her end up with Johnny, who hits her when he's drunk.

The loneliness that follows this is immense. Black women feel as if they have to choose between finding a diamond among fool's gold or they'll be condemned to a life of isolation. Isolation follows depression, due to a lack of support and community from those who told her that they only want what's best for her. "Who am I if not with a man?" As if it's impossible to find communion and love by other methods.

The reason I call it the "loneliness lie" is because it's exactly that. Loneliness has been a scam sold to women globally as a method of control and weakened thinking. Loneliness in the context of being a threat against women who want better lives for themselves leaves out how women have sought and gained positive dynamics with other women. Many black women, I believe, would benefit from focusing on their friendships with other women and turning their focus from solely finding love to finding their voice in the world. Not one woman has ever been ruined by a lack of romantic interest, but all women have much to gain from female connection.

If love is defined as control and dominance over a submissive, then that idea of "love" must be destroyed for true love to be prioritized and to encompass multiple factors. Romantic love shouldn't be viewed as the sole valid way to give and receive love, when love can be between friends, family, or love towards oneself. To reform the structure of romantic love from a control structure, we must eliminate the idea that it's the only form of love that exists. For women, black women especially, to gain equal respect between two minds, the idea that one mind must dull her voice and 1concerns to remain with the other mind must be thrown away. Love being shown as romantic, friendly, and familial will then be seen as the norm, rather than a rarity for black women.

*Inspired by the writings of Audre Lorde

# Abuse and Resilience: Discussion Questions

Use these questions to spark conversation about the poems, stories, and essays in this section.

## Funny, In Hindsight

by Quan Williams

1. The narrator decided to tell us a story about how she was abused as a child from a more humorous perspective. How did that impact your perception of the abuse?

2. What does the reader learn about the mandated reporter and social service system that is supposed to protect the child?

3. From this brief account, we learn that abuse happened several times. Instead of taking the child away from the mother, should attending long-term counseling and mental health monitoring be a requirement for the child to stay in the home?

4. How do you think the parent feels about the story? Should it matter?

---

## Father's Death

by George Hammons

1. In this poem, we learn that the speaker's father was "suspected" of murder on more than one occasion. He physically abused his wife, and from the story, he was going to murder the mother. What was your emotional response to the mother's reprieve from being murdered and the actions she took afterward?

2. How does the poet capture the feeling of complete abandonment in an abusive household?

2. Do you agree with the aunt about the eulogy?

## Home

by George Hammons

1. This poem seems to be a variation of what happened on that fateful night in *Father's Death*, or it is another chilling experience of the father's abuse. What is not said is just as important as what is said in this poem. Since the children didn't talk about it and confirm it with each other, and talk about how they felt, do you think they all have similar memories of the abuse?

---

## On the Bus

by George Hammons

1. What do you think is going on with this bus ride and the emotions of the child on the bus? Do you think he is processing the abuse in the house?

---

## Moonslick

by Eric DeVaughnn

1. What emotions does this poem evoke for you? How does the poet accomplish this? Do you feel empathy for the mother and the son? It is described as a familiar ritual we are used to; does this make it more acceptable or tragic, and why?

---

## The Wound I Won't Stop Touching

by Angelique Zobitz

1. Do you think the narrator in this poem is victimizing the victim or working towards healing and accountability?

2. Does there seem to be hope for healing for the speaker in the poem, or does the person feel trapped?

## Drawn to Abusive Men in My Youth

by Jasmine Vallejo-Love

1. What does this poem have in common with *The Wound I Won't Stop Touching*? Do you think the speaker in Drawn to Abusive Men is still in abusive relationships?

---

## You Never Laid a Hand on Me

by Jasmine Vallejo-Love

1. How does this poem describe emotional abuse and its lingering impact?

2. How does the end of this poem mirror the quote at the beginning of this section?

---

## Corpus Delicti

by Stephanie Liggins

1. What violence occurred in the story?

2. Is there anything anyone could or should have done? What would you do?

3. Why does the author start and end the poem with a stanza of poetry?

4. What is ironic in the story, and how does the irony focus the reader's attention on the crime?

5. Why is the story entitled *Corpus Delicti* (body of the crime or evidence showing that the act was the result of a crime, not an accident or natural event)?

---

## Black Women's Loneliness Crisis

by Amaya Marshall

1. Do you agree or disagree with the author's premise that *women have been wired by patriarchal constraints to center our lives on finding love*?

2. Do you think her aversion to this is a result of the abuse she has witnessed?

3. According to a study by the Institute for Women's Policy Research, "more than four in ten Black women experience physical abuse from an intimate partner during their lifetimes. Black women also experience significantly higher rates of psychological abuse—including humiliation, insults, name-calling, and coercive control—than do women overall."[1] In 2023, 733 Black females were murdered by males in single victim/single offender incidents at a rate of 3.1 per 100,000.[2] How might this information impact a young Black woman and her desire to be in a relationship?

4. Why do you think people stay with abusive partners?

5. How could counseling help a person coming out of a long-term abusive relationship?

# Diagnosed But Not Defined

Mental Health problems don't define who we are.
They are something you experience.
You walk in the rain, and you feel the rain,
but you are not the rain.

—Matt Haig

*In some ways, I see this as a snapshot of the African American experience within the United States. There are obstacles and stereotypes that we each must overcome, yet the resilient souls of the people will always shine.*

– Ipyani Lockert, photographer

# Angel Cherise Alley

Depression /Anxiety

Interview with Angel Cherise Alley

**Interviewer**: How old were you when you received your diagnosis?

**Angel**: I was thirty-five years old when I received help, but I first started showing signs of depression and anxiety. I received my first diagnosis when I was thirteen. However, my mother ignored the diagnosis from the doctor, stating, "She has nothing to be stressed or depressed about." Therefore, I continued without assistance, perpetually misunderstood and criticized as "too sensitive" or labeled "a brat."

**Interviewer**: How has it impacted your life?

**Angel**: Yikes! It's been an up-and-down battle. Sometimes I've stayed in bed for longer than what was healthy. I've had suicidal ideation. Thankfully, my aunt heard me say "I am tired," and urged my mother to get me help. My father came. That diverted the attempt. I sought therapy for myself when I was 22. I've seen several therapists since then; I'm now 52. I've participated in group therapy and was assigned to a program (not in-house), which I attended for approximately 3 weeks daily. I was unable to work. I've learned many different ways to care for myself. I've read books like "Boundaries" and listened to experts or thought leaders. I keep pursuing my healing.

**Interviewer**: What do you want to tell the audience?

**Angel**: Unapologetically care for yourself. It's OK to take care of yourself. **Admitting you need help is courageous**. There are many helpful, healthful people and communities. Although you may not be receiving the response from loved ones you expect, some are unable or incapable of giving us what we need or hope for. Nonetheless, people and communities are available to listen and offer you a lifeline. Expand your love line and stay connected to caring communities.

*Angel Cherise Alley - Depression/Anxiety*

# Joseph M. Page

Schizoaffective, Severe Depression, Bipolar, PTSD

Interview with Joseph Mekael Page

**Interviewer**: How old were you when you received your diagnosis?

**Joseph**: I received the diagnosis of bipolar, schizoaffective, severe depression, and PTSD in 2025.

**Interviewer**: How has it impacted your life?

**Joseph**: It's been a journey, no doubt. Today, things are much more stable. The rough edges have been ironed out, and I understand myself better than ever before. Therapy — especially group therapy — has been a real anchor. It keeps my head clear, my spirit grounded, and my focus aligned with the things I love to do.

Being dual-diagnosed means navigating both mental-health challenges and substance-use history. There are still tough moments, but nothing I can't overcome. I've been fighting through it, and I'm still standing.

In the early stages, before I understood my diagnosis, everything hit a lot harder. I didn't have the language for what I was experiencing. But now that I know my symptoms and triggers, I can respond differently. I can recognize when my mind or my impulses are pulling me in the wrong direction — and I choose to go the opposite way. I choose stability. I choose clarity. I choose to act in alignment with the person I know I am becoming.

**Interviewer**: What do you want to tell the reading audience, or what do you hope they will learn from you?

**Joseph**: I hope that they learned that you are not what your diagnosis is and that people might fear you because they don't understand you. It's ok, just keep being kind and showing love, everything will work out just the way it should.

*Joseph M. Page - Schizoaffective, Severe Depression, Bipolar, PTSD*

# We Are a Quilt

If you (or someone you care about)
cannot take on as much as someone else,
that does not make you either weak or crazy.
You just have to prepare differently
and live your life unapologetically for you.

– Rheeda Walker

# Medicine is the Best Medicine

Model & Photographer: Alora Young

# Ode to My Antidepressants

by Alora Young

i have a confession to make,
it's not queer,
actually, i am queer.
but that's not the confession we're here for
as a poet, i need to keep this like a secret,
but for the first time, i'm happy.
my chemical imbalance in all its bitter malice
has been tamed.
and i haven't been the same since i met
fluvoxamine.

the word just rolls off your tongue
and it fills me with,
not love but awe.
and honestly, i never thought i would feel this way about
a girl,
i mean pill.
i take it home with me and keep it in my bedside drawer.
at first, my parents didn't approve of it
she's a little lab-grown,
synthetic kind of friend,
but in the end, they came around.
because they found out she,
it, knew how to make them happy too.
and now we all have chemical embellishments
of varying relevance that takes great precedence.

overall other things i pack for vacation
(six pairs of underwear and ten vyvanses, minimum)
i feel like the bobcat that had clawed
its way into my chest has finally been evicted.
it was not paying rent; we had to go to court.
it was ugly, but paliperidone is a great lawyer.

now we take life as a team, me and hydroxyzine,
and I've never been happier.
for the first time, my skin feels like it sits right
atop my muscles and bone.
and me and all my medically prescribed friends
are finally at home.

my pills are a prophecy
for a life i long to live,
a world that i honestly

wasn't sure that god would give.
my mind is finally healing
from all i have survived.
all this has left me reeling
wide awake and alive.

every morning i choose happiness.
every evening i choose peace.
medicine is the best medicine
to tame a mental beast.
i will take fluvoxamine like the eucharist,
the brilliant and the flawed,
the healed and the humanist,
the image of our god.
i will take my daily pills,

and my daily bread.
i will soothe the scared child
that lives inside my head.
i will peer into the future to see all i now can be
and i will be happy to realize
all i have to be
is a better me.

# Obsessive Compulsive Personality Disorder

by Akilah Brown

I had been seeing my therapist for three years before she used the term OCPD which stands for obsessive-compulsive personality disorder, one of the most prevalent but least talked about personality disorders. Before that, when she said I was obsessive-compulsive, I thought she meant I had OCD, obsessive-compulsive disorder, which I definitely do not, so when I looked up OCD symptoms, I always shrugged the obsessive-compulsive description off. But OCPD is a completely different kettle of fish from OCD. Someone with OCPD is a rigid rule follower with a high moral code and severe perfectionism who has problems with personal relationships. I'm paraphrasing and simplifying, of course, but that gets to the heart of the matter. The cause is (shocker!) linked to childhood trauma, specifically verbal and emotional abuse via constant criticism, so that the child thinks perfect = safe.

People with OCPD don't think they have a problem, so they are hard to treat. As someone who hates therapy–and doesn't trust anyone who likes it–I was amused when I started researching the disorder and saw the need for order and structure listed as a caution for mental health professionals. I hate/resist the unpredictability of therapy and I have always treated therapy like a roller coaster: it might have an emotional up or down, but the track is laid and set, and I know what to expect. However, my current therapist is very good at her job, so I would go in with something I wanted to talk about, like an encounter I had at work. Then we would somehow wind up talking about an experience from my childhood or young adulthood that caused me emotional distress. I would end each session saying how much I hate therapy, then start the next session still angry that it went off the rails the week before, and would have a new plan for how to make sure the session followed the path I wanted. Then, it would go in some unexpected direction again. After a few weeks of this, I would square my shoulders and tell my therapist, "No, I'm committed to this. I want to get better, and I know this will help. I will feel my feelings." Yet, still, I would find myself pissed off at the end, like my therapist had somehow tricked me into addressing something I didn't plan to.

Given all of that, it may not be surprising that emotional expression and feeling feelings are challenges for people with OCPD. During each session, my therapist will ask me what emotions I'm feeling (I often have to refer to a list) and what physical sensations I'm feeling. My research also shows that "the outcome for people with OCPD is generally better when they have a good understanding of their condition" (Rizvi & Torrico). This is part of why I was surprised my therapist didn't mention my diagnosis for so long or give me a heads up that when I have such a visceral physical response, it's probably the disorder.

To be fair, sometimes my whole life feels like an OCPD episode, which makes sense since, by definition, a personality disorder means a persistent pattern of behavior.

With OCPD specifically, the pattern includes perfectionism, rigidity, and control that detrimentally affects a person's quality of life. It also usually shows up in young adulthood, which tracks with my experience, considering I had my daughter at nineteen and, at twenty-five, moved from Maryland to Iowa (1,000+ miles away from my support system) to attend graduate school. Rigidity and control were necessary to manage my schooling as well as my daughter's. Schedules needed to be attended to, childcare needed to be arranged, and safety was paramount. I didn't have time for feelings since there was work to be done and a household to manage. Also, I was making such a big change that it needed to be worth our while, which meant doing a good job — perhaps a perfect one? — in graduate school. Those traits served me well then, for logistical purposes, but do not so much now.

Once I fully understood what OCPD is, it made me sad. I already knew and accepted I had a mental illness because I had been previously diagnosed with depression. OCPD is a Cluster C or anxiety-based personality disorder. When it came to anxiety, before I was aware of my diagnosis, I liked to stay in denial about it, even as I would tell my friends that I recognized perfectionism as a type of anxiety. And by "stay in denial," that means I usually referred to myself as a recovering perfectionist and my anxiety as "the anxiety I don't admit to having," which was my way of saying that I was slowly on the road to acceptance.

Honestly, I think it's the knowledge that OCPD is a response to verbal abuse that made me sad. Living with a highly critical parent is a particularly insidious form of abuse because, for me, I can see how the criticism was supposed to help. It's hard, even still, to use the word abusive to describe the way I grew up, but the OCPD didn't just come from nowhere. It came from a steady stream of feedback that what I did and how I was wasn't good enough. It also came from a steady stream of feedback about what my friends did, and how they weren't good enough either; somehow, I was responsible for that, too. Growing up, I believed that if people would just act right, then things would be okay, so I forced myself to act right so I could be okay. I also fully acknowledge that I am a rule follower and chronic good girl, so nothing about the actual description of the symptoms was surprising or new, except for knowing it's a personality disorder and bona fide mental illness.

In preparation for this essay, I asked my therapist when she realized that OCPD was my diagnosis. She was reluctant to tell me because when I got diagnosed with Major Depressive Disorder, I went into a rage spiral (an essay for another time, perhaps). After I assured her it was just to get an accurate timeline, she said it became obvious within a few months that she was treating me for OCPD.

Today, I can acknowledge that treatment is working. Therapy isn't so hard anymore, and I can't remember the last time I shut down in session or complained about how much I hated it. I still don't like surprises, I still hate uncertainty, I still want people to follow the rules, I still have high moral standards, and I still make backup plans for my backup plans. I don't see any of those things changing–at least, not yet. However, I'm able to stop and assess my feelings, to pay attention to my bodily responses, and to sit in the discomfort of those feelings for longer periods. It's also easier to see when I'm using disordered thinking so that I can stop and get out of my own way. That progress gives me hope, as well as a name for why I am the way I am. Now that I know I have OCPD, I have language to describe the behaviors I engage in, and, especially, why I often react to things the way I do. For that, I'm grateful.

*See Page 234

# Panic Attack: On the Edge of Oblivion

by Angelique DeVonish

It starts with a throb.

Before I can brace myself,
the floor gives way
and I sink into the nightmare.

My heart speeds up its arrhythmic drumming
in my ear
turning up the volume.
Not so much a song,
as a warning,
*I'm going to stop in a second.*

Dread tries to bear its face.

I scream,
pressing hands against skull
as if to squeeze out the panic.

I moan,
regretfully closing my eyes.

Dumb move.

In the dark
I run the risk
of tumbling into the abyss.

Tiptoeing on its ledge,
Arms sprawled out
Leaning against the deteriorating wall of my marbles
I breathlessly watch them fall into the black
one by one
and hear a voice echo back,

*You're going crazy.*

A fate worse than death.

I open my lids as fast as I can
and move.

*Keep moving,*
*you got this.*
*Touch ground.*
*I'm here.*
*There is nothing to fear,*
I repeat until my voice holds true.
Fighting tooth and nail
against the counter energy,
gunning for my soul.

Finally!

Stride catches in sync with heart
and I return to some semblance of normalcy.

# Underneath It All

by Dana I. Hunter

I can feel my taut skin like the
covering of a breaching whale
nudging its way to break surface

I feel it twisting beneath.
It's frightening at times
and I fear it as much as you.

My breaching whale is hidden
underneath a membrane of medication.
Pharmaceutical protection, from a final escape.

I am grateful for medicinal magic.

It's something that can control
a mind which has a will of its own.
Underneath it all is a violent and turbulent sea.

I am fine and feel safe
as long as I remember
and am aware of its existence

underneath it all.

# Neurotic Animation

by Mervyn Seivwright

I feel flares through curtain fissures
strike me from slumber, my mind
running to catch the last car on a train.
My brain, a pulsating core of a steam engine

chugging with a crescendo. Despite
achieved goals written on a poster board
centered on my bedroom wall, falling
short of society's expectations, flunking

fatherhood, years of forfeited finances,
melanin not matching chess pieces in play,
I lash my back to wipe out sins of failure.
It's not enough. While I do

not serve my heart, an overripe peach
ill-tended, worried about the rest
of the orchard around me, my words
are tangled seaweed, the gavel of judgment

slams when my mouth opens, when words
play hide and keep hiding bubbling
oxygen while rising just shy
of the sea's surface, I want to stop

the train in my head along loose tracks
bend to the left, then right,
a London Underground tube
speeding turn, crying out in a canyon,

I want to sleep.
My fated thread is thin,
steady, not ready to be cut.
I won't cut it.

I can't falter, scratching sound
screeches the blackboard.
The rules have vanished. The chalk
is rubbed out—I linger.

# Attention-Deficit / Hyperactivity Disorder

by Romaine Washington

ADHD is one of the most common neurodevelopmental disorders. According to 2023 data from the CDC and recent studies, an estimated 15.5 million adults in the U.S. (roughly 6.0%) have a current ADHD diagnosis, and more than half were diagnosed in adulthood.[1] Black children are often punished for their behavior and labeled as troublemakers or lazy, and they are misdiagnosed. Black females are the least diagnosed. There are many symptoms, but the most basic are included in the diagnosis title and behavior, and are characterized by inattention, hyperactivity, or both.

**Do I have ADHD?** If you suspect that you may have ADHD, there are online tests you can take along with lists of symptoms. However, to ensure you are properly assessed and diagnosed, it is wise to see a primary care doctor and/or a therapist.

**Executive Dysfunction:** People with executive dysfunction struggle to organize and regulate their behavior in ways that will help them accomplish long-term goals. **Symptoms can vary in severity**, especially if there is another co-occurring condition such as anxiety or depression.[2]

**H**yperactivity/**H**yperfocus? The **H** in ADHD can present as **hyperactivity**, but it can also present as **hyperfocus**, referring to prolonged, intense concentration on tasks of high interest. This focus can lead to productive work but also to negative outcomes, such as missed deadlines or personal neglect.[3]

**How the ADHD Brain Reacts**: The "Four Fs" of ADHD—Fight, Flight, Freeze, and Fib (or Fawn)—represent common, often subconscious, stress responses to overwhelming situations, emotional dysregulation, or rejection sensitivity.[4]

**Treatment and Support**

Treatment and support can reduce symptoms and improve functioning. Psychotherapy, cognitive behavioral therapy (CBT), ADHD coaching, using various strategies such as planners, setting reminders, and building consistent routines, are all helpful, and in some cases, medication may help.[5] If you have ADHD, please know that your symptoms are just that, symptoms of brain-based challenges. They are not moral shortcomings, excuses, or character flaws. There is help available to help you manage.

1)"Facts About ADHD in Adults." (11 October 2024). Retrieved May 09, 2026. https://www.cdc.gov/adhd/php/adults/index.html
2)Janice Rodden. "Executive Dysfunction? Signs and Symptoms of EFD." (@ October 2025). Retrieved May 11, 2026. https://www.additudemag.com/what-is-executive-function-disorder/?srsltid=AfmBOoq52tE_gZeBpfB7f1nO0qOwO55BHxwhoriop6RR8U7-ChGlj97E#what-is-executive-dysfunction
3) Grigore T. Popa. "Hyperfocus in ADHD: A Misunderstood Cognitive Phenomenon." (26 August 2025). Retrieved May 09, 2026. https://pmc.ncbi.nlm.nih.gov/articles/PMC12437476/
4) Monica Hassall, R.N., and Barbara Hunter, M.Ed. "ADDitude. Fight, Flight, Freeze...or Fib?" (11 August 2025). Retrieved May 11, 2026. https://www.additudemag.com/why-lie-adhd-fight-flight
5) National Institute of Mental Health. "U. S. Department of Health and Human Services, ADHD in Adults: 4 Things to Know." (2024). Retrieved May 09, 2026. https://www.nimh.nih.gov/health/publications/adhd-what-you-need-to-know

# Response Time

by Matthew E. Henry

they say it takes eight to ten years
before knowing dark clouds
soak only your shoulders.

that anger laps its serrated tongue
within your ears alone.

that the weighted blanket of sorrow
constricting your chest
is uncommon bed clothes.

that no one else has named
a monster who holds, is held, tighter
than an infant's teddy bear.

eight to ten years between knowing
the above—seeing the fire by day,
the arrows at night—and asking
for help to quell them both.
let us talk about time travel.

# Hoarder's Quilt

by Lydia Theon Ware i

How do you make a quilt out of the scraps from a pre-hoarder's pile of filthy rags? Do you handwash each strip in bleach, lemon juice, and vinegar to get the stains out, and mask the smell? Or do you wait 'til it's done, piece sewn into piece, clean thread holding taut the linen of forgotten moments, of pierced skin nightmares, of jumbled new beginnings. Making a quilt from your past.

What is a quilt but hand-me-downs you seek to remember?

Quilting is a necessity, a sharing of one's legacy, blending one's past and future. When the material for the quilt is not the pile of hoarded overflowing clothing that some consider rubbish, when the material of the quilt being constructed is made from your brain cells recovering from mental illness, then the truth of what filth really is becomes even more blurry.

Predatory thoughts, thoughts of self-harm, thoughts of self-hatred, do they become the border scraps that support the pattern of wellness that has to layer the top? Or do you discard them, piece by piece - replace them with new scraps, clean thread, holding together the memory of what you always knew could be?

Quilts of flesh and blood are impossible to create, but quilts of the mental illness journey, that can begin with a question: what is your sanest thought? If sunflowers can be grown from bugs and soil, then why can't mental wellness be grown from the soil of psychosis?

# Being Bipolar

by Jasmine Vallejo-Love

There is absolutely nothing wrong.
*Really*.

Good job. Some say amazing.
Decent health. Physical and emotional pain, but tolerable.
Loving/caring/loyal/respectable husband, albeit too jovial.
A cute homeowner, not a renter, to grow old in.
A non-yappy dog.
Parents, alive, well, 3,000 miles away for a reason.
Friends, many, some like family, some for decoration.

There is absolutely nothing wrong.
*Really*.

Except sometimes

the world is without its color,
there's yearning for "feelings" that can't be reached,
a wonder if they'll come,
if their existence was real,
and in that limbo,
death seems easier

but orchestrating it would take too much effort.
I want nothing but sleep.

Activities of daily living neglected.
Can't worry about consequences –
social life non-existent,
career possibly stalled,
partner feels ignored.

There is absolutely nothing wrong.
*Really*.

Except other times

My eyes can't rest.
Hues as vibrant as a psilocybin-induced altered reality,
blinding whites, blood reds, boundless blues.

Brain waves overload,
thoughts shoot like wild bullets from a machine gun,
as casings hit the pavement,
the little clinks, lost tidbits of memories.

Then everything needs to align.
The curtains ironed,
books in size order,
wine by maker and grape, and year,
closet, pantry, kitchen, office – torn apart and reset.
At work – organized and hyper productive.

And then there is absolutely nothing wrong.
*Really.*

As suddenly as it begins, it ends.
Air tastes crisp.
The shine on the hardwood floors is a reminder of its luxury.
On the drive to work, the SoCal scenery brings a smile and a tear.
The sound of his voice is a relief. He's chosen to be here, again.
My family of friends fills the crevices, and the role
of matriarch is resumed – provider, therapist, negotiator.

The Trips are just another quirk.
Everybody has one at least,
or so we like to say.

# Schizophrenia, anyone?

By Lydia Theon Ware i

It's been 28 years.
Does she remember the steps to curiosity and creation?
What she does remember is that God made laughter
just for her and He is a tickler.

For 28 years, she knew the rules of Sanity
complete with proper papers,
boredom, but better
because there is ease at the end of the day,
Emboldened fruit-filled possibilities,
a cat curled into contented sleep,
and a yellow stretch of hope.

It's been twenty-eight years

obliterated by raging meteors,
hard to pay attention
when your mind wants to detonate reality.

Have you ever lost your mind?
It feels like a team of players on the field
has lost the rules of the game,
running around, back and forth,
without a way to score,
and no one recognizes the ball.

Have you ever been Insane?
It feels like the world doesn't add up
and the math on the chalkboard
refuses to make sense.
Word problems read in gibberish,
Internal dialogue is spilled whispers
and hidden wind lulled into crevices
of buried unfamiliar music.
Insanity is like soft flesh
broken into a prickly rash.
It's playing tennis with live ammo,
Bleak booms with each fumbled lob
against a flaming net.

It's hard to pay attention
when your mind wants to detonate reality.

She had been both Sane and Insane.

For twenty-eight years she was a seesaw
careening from Sane thoughts to wild delusions.
Pills and injections and therapy took away the crazy,
and returned her mind to the almost original.

Sanity is boulders ceasing to be
exercise equipment.
Sanity is love.
Sanity is being able to breathe
Sanity is no longer expecting
the golden thread to unravel.

# Wading

by Dana I. Hunter

I find myself swimming
in uncharted moods.
If life revolved with me
instead of against the tide
this journey would unfold
as a billowing wave.

Once again, I am wadding
in a pool of possibilities,
as droplets of hope linger
on tips of toes, slowly
dripping to form a shallow pool.

Maybe a year from now
I will be able to dive in
and swim.

# Sounds of Broken Glass

by Brittany Miles

It was quiet time. That window between finished weekend errands and dinner. Mom's moment of silence, if you will. While adjusting the pillows for my back, I heard her before she arrived. Layla, my four-year-old daughter, stood at the door of my sanctuary, better known as Mama's room.

"What's up, Bug?"

"Mama, did you hear it?

"Hear what?" The house was mostly silent this day.

"The glass, Mama, I thought you broke some glass."

"Ah," pretending I understood. "No. No glass."

"Okay. Bye, Mama."

She ran down the hall to start Barbie's next adventure. I listened to her animated storytelling to her dolls, while a Barbie movie played full blast. These were the sounds of our home. It was one of those times I wondered what she was talking about. I decided to dismiss this as a typical little kid conversation.

These moments became more of the norm. "Did you call me Mama?" she'd ask when I was a few feet away from her in the kitchen. "No, Bug, I didn't," I'd say, part of me wondering if she was just trying to be obedient. That's not unusual among young girls, I thought while I carefully chopped onions for tonight's dinner.

All these questions and doubts swirled uneasily in my spirit. Was this her wild childhood imagination or something else? Am I making something innocent into something it's not?

I remember reading about a young girl in the L.A. Times named Jani who had childhood schizophrenia. Layla was around her age when I read the piece, and I couldn't help but wonder. There were similarities between the girls, and I tucked that inside me. That memory stayed with me as I didn't understand what was going on with my daughter, but it felt eerily familiar. That girl couldn't function at school or at home. Layla went to school and never had a tantrum in her life. Perhaps this is not what it is.

Through elementary school, the voices became louder and stronger. The voices, innocuous at first, started to complicate our lives.

Layla was a skinny girl and a picky eater. It was difficult to eat with Layla. I was constantly begging her to eat. She never seemed to like any of my food. Dinnertime was playtime to her; she'd walk away from the table, ignoring the fast-chilling food, and find a toy to play with. Bargaining was a challenge, but it worked sometimes. My dinner, cold and inedible, went into the trash. Later, I learned that watching the Disney Channel with a tray and me with a glass of Merlot worked best.

Every Wednesday, I got her favorite, McDonald's. Her Happy Meals consisted of 6-piece nuggets, of which she would eat half along with a handful of fries. I was puzzled as to why she refused to eat. Her pediatrician had ruled out any medical reason and told me she was just picky. Still, something about it felt wrong—it wasn't just pickiness; there was something different about Layla's behavior.

Layla told me years later that the voices warned her that my food was poisonous and recommended that she not eat it. While McDonald's was her favorite, the voices said that it could kill her, too.

The voices frightened her at times. Nightmares were commonplace. Sleeping in my bed became the norm. Before I tucked her in, she'd tell me someone was trying to break in. We lived in a townhome with three levels, so I understood her fear. I told her, "We have a security system. You've seen it on the wall and watched me push the buttons plenty of times. It's okay, Bug, it's okay." Usually, she was not convinced. I read in bed until it was time to watch Housewives. Layla gently snored. I felt a darkness coming over us.

Layla started to miss milestones. While working with a neuropsychologist, I searched for issues like dyslexia. Sure enough, he diagnosed Layla with dyslexia and ADHD. That was the answer. Case closed. But there was something off. She still feared food, heard weird sounds, and had paranoia. I saw specialist after specialist looking for the answer, each one missing the bigger picture.

Then, in third grade, when Layla started refusing to go to school almost every day, I began considering mental health. Each day, there was a battle to get her shoes, parka, and backpack on and get in the car.

Despite being popular and at the center of her friends' group, she detested going. Why so much commotion every morning? Many days, I kept her home with me while I worked remotely as best I could. This disruption was impacting my work. The school called too.

I didn't know what to do, but the voices did. Layla kept telling me someone was trying to kidnap her. I accused her of lying and insisted she get in the car.

While tears streamed down her face, we would frantically rush into the drop-off line just before the bell rang. Bathing also became a battle, and it was difficult to get her clean. Dirt was visible on her tiny neck. I'd send her back to the shower to bathe until I was satisfied. By the time she turned eleven, she started developing grandiose delusions. Layla was claiming to be Jesus Christ to her classmates. Her friends laughed it off and thought she was a lovable, weird kid. Recently, I asked why she didn't tell me about the delusion, and she said she thought I knew.

Shock didn't cover my reaction; it was more like devastation. How could I have missed this, of all things?

My motherly intuition was signaling that something was deeply wrong, but I lacked the vocabulary to discuss the situation with family or friends. I kept thinking it was something other than it was.

I was unsure (afraid) how to approach her. Layla, for her part, believed everyone could hear voices. She was a child; how would she know differently? Voices were a core part of her inner world. If she didn't tell me directly, I couldn't ask more questions about her experience. Even if I believed her, most doctors would say she'd outgrow it.

I felt fear and realized that my options were becoming more limited, leading me down a path I didn't want to take. I had to relinquish control and submit to the truth. Mental illness was the culprit; it was time for a medical evaluation. Luckily, I found her psychiatrist, through a co-worker whom she sees to this day. He diagnosed Layla with schizophrenia. He had confirmed my deepest fears.

The signs of my failure as a mother were glaring. I didn't see this coming. This wasn't something kids got, right? As Dr. Mom, I prepared my medicine cabinet for bumps, bruises, and blood. Sure, kids got depressed and anxious, but I never thought my child would have schizophrenia. From her doctor, I learned it's the most serious mental illness, and only .01% of children are diagnosed with the disease.

Scared but open, I could relate to having a mental illness. My depression has been ongoing since I was a teenager. There are still days I can't function; those are my down days, as Layla calls them. In the African American community, there's stigma, which is why I don't talk about it much. We were taught as kids to keep going no matter what and to count our blessings. Psychic pain was a luxury we Black folk couldn't afford. It's my secret, like the voices.

Schizophrenia was new to me. Layla was hearing and soon started seeing things that weren't there, like hairy slugs in my closet, people in the sky, and moving walls. Things got rough for her around the age of eleven. That's when we admitted her to Seattle Children's Hospital Psychiatric and Behavioral Medicine Unit for five days. She spent time learning how to silence the whispers and the moving walls. I thought she'd be cured. Once home, we waited and waited. The cure never came.

Layla is seventeen years old and still hears the voices, sees sky people, and is paranoid. She didn't move beyond it, and it didn't get better. What I learned is to heed the still, small voice inside of you. No matter how devastating it is to your heart, listen. On one particularly hopeless day, Layla reminded me, "Mama, the voices won't ever stop." My spine quivered, confirming she was right.

What I've learned is that I can be here for Layla; I can't envision her world, the shattering glass, the whispers, or the sky people, but I can hold her hand or give her a hug.

Sometimes we cry together when the nights are long and harrowing. And sometimes, it feels as if there's no one in the world but the two of us. Isolated and alone, but together. Often, I remind her that we didn't get this far just to get this far. Enclosing her in a mama bear hug, I gently stroke her teary cheeks, and she smiles knowingly.

My maternal blueprint was shattered by childhood schizophrenia. But I've learned a lot from it, and it's made me a resilient and compassionate mother. Schizophrenia is an old friend who's welcome in our home. It sits in a closet, watching and waiting. We don't ignore it; we pay attention to its signs. I made peace with it. It's nothing to be feared or reviled. Even though schizophrenia came uninvited, it brought the gift of being Layla's mom.

# Mother

by Jasmine Vallejo-Love

She is bipolar.

Unlike the earth rotating
forever in a defined orbit,
she spins off cycle.
Fast and blurry

then s l o w s

stops only once
to wink at me,
her eyes batting
like a solar eclipse.

Proving for just a second,
her mind is not completely gone.
I get warm fuzzies
and wait patiently, even years

for the right side of the pole.

# Comfort.

Model and Photographer: Alora Young

# Light Switch

by Beverly George

Light switches off, disrobes the dark,
I call my daughter
In this hospital room but she answers not as the cold draft
Assumes I'll abandon her

On the edge of her bed, I desperately try to understand
Stories describing a patchwork quilt
Stitched with promises of a man
She loved just a little too much just last spring.

As we "talk" we thumb through a cardboard shoebox
Of faded photos of her childhood before my divorce
Tying threads together from the unraveled past
My frayed nerves buffering every loaded

Response until she whispers under her breath
"I love you, Mom,"
Cold draft relents, quilt squares realign like puzzle pieces
Patiently reassigned.

I embrace her thin frame and feel
Her warm arms take hold,
Not knowing how, or for how long
She'll keep her light switched on.

# The intrusive self-awareness posed by a long day of avoiding responsibilities in a fruitless attempt to ward off the pressing urge to simply give up, lie down, and cry

by Alora Young

I know I am depressed when I feel
the itch in my fingers to write a poem,

to crack myself open upon the seams
like a gourd,
all lumps and carbuncles,
a smooth seam from the teeth of a machete.

And I dig around in the halves of me
for the answer to the doubt,
for the clock that pervades all I am
with a temperamentally ticking
bomb it is undoubtedly attached to.

I am a new kind of person,
a schizophrenic who camps out in classrooms,
instead of asylums,
with an old school kind of brilliance.
The dark, meddlesome kind
for 20-year-old geniuses who die by 30.
I persist in living.

I will be accepting congratulations on behalf
of a series of chemical compounds,
the most exciting of which being
one Mr. Paliperidone and his wife, Fluvoxamine.

They say the first sign of society is a healed femur,

that we know people civilized themselves when
the sick, do not simply get left behind to die.
In a civilized country my mother wiped my forehead
as I cried, nearly catatonic, paralyzed by delusions
and demonic spirits.

Every day I wear a face upon my face
that fronts like the brain behind it does not
have teeth.

That it does not
gnaw at itself like my psyche is an arm
stuck under a boulder,
and that arm is the only thing standing between
me, and dying painfully alone.

I have been tended to very gently,
but my beloved classrooms do not
have room for a fragile Id.
I keep it hidden.
I was not made for the pressure.
I'm emotionally winded,
been running so long
I feel like I'm breathing through a straw.

In the absence of myself,
in the char black gulf of anxiety
I doggy paddled through,
I clipped my nails too low,
and now they hurt when i pick things up.

I am haunted by incessant clicking
with no origin.
The pain in my fingertips surge
as I dig into my ears
for a mortal silence.

It is a soft reminder of my human flesh.
Despite how I dream myself
to be superhuman and immortal

I am a fragile thing,

a stick of room-temperature butter on a counter
crushed by a toddler's sinking fingers.
A consciousness that lurks
like a sour taste in the mouth.

# Cracked

by Alexander James

HD had finally had enough.
His home had become a pressure cooker,
and he was this close to cracking.

Men know when they are walking on eggshells.
One mistake with the wife and
the argument won't be over easy.

For HD, his sunny side never turned up.
Always too runny.
He felt like he was always running.

But every day, he hid in his shell.
He would cover his face and cheese.
His soft-boiled wife was the only one that did not see
how scrambled he was.

A man can only omelet so much.
I mean fold so much.
I mean hold so much.
He told himself
if you're not at the table, you're on the menu.

Though he worked for the King,
he always felt poached.

The King had money, men and horses.
But they never fixed anything.

HD was convinced
the time for his big break had passed.
His gift was spoiled.

He felt forced into shapes he hated.
No one to open up to,
his thoughts became deviled.

His heart is salty.
What do you expect when you compare yourself
to those who are cage-free?

Until one day,
instead of climbing into bed,
he climbed up a wall.

They never found out why
he did it.

# on monday, poet's head sang and hurt

by Jordan E. Franklin

*After "Last Night a DJ Saved My Life" by Indeep*

Last time my mouth spilled, I was buckled into an ambulance.
Night was too cold. A doctor wanted to fix my bad brain.

Awake, the night was cold. A doctor couldn't fix my brain.
DJ spun songs through me so I wouldn't think those thoughts again.

"Saved," those songs spun through me so I couldn't think again.
My skull held a gray traitor. I was too sick to dance.

Life gave me a gray traitor. I was too sick to dance.
From day to hour, I pretended. I continued to be unwell.

Another day, another hour, I pretended. I tried to be well.
Broken brain stretched out for years on the road behind me.

Heart heaving, my brain stretched out for years behind me.
Inside was too cold. A doctor wanted to but couldn't fix my brain.

Night was too cold. A doctor couldn't fix my bad brain.
Last time my mouth spilled, I was buckled into an ambulance.

# Seventy-two Hours by Ginger M. Galloway

The
Rattle of keys
Heavy footsteps
Green cotton coordinates
Nurse's scrubs
Misplaced
Shoes without laces
He says it reminds him of jail
Heavy doors
Keeping them safe
For now
And a cocktail of antidepressants
In little shot glass cups
She won't
Talk
To us
Clinical
A group session of
s
  t
    r
      i
        n
          g
            i
              n
                g beads
Art therapy
L    o    n        g
Deep
Breaths
Clouds dissipate in the air in front of lips
That won't
Talk
Just a bout of diarrhea
Watch for signs of
Depression
The drugs for depression
Causing...
I'm her roommate
We decorated our room

It's too bad
It's so pretty
You can't see it
Smiling and laughter
Card flipping
And flapping birds
The shuffling suits
Cries that echo in the hall
There's no windows
In the walls' painted
Beach
Everyone ignores the noise
She's new
Having a crisis
That's what they call it
A crisis
One doctor for the floor
Who only comes
Like a wave
Once a day
Pushing in
Quickly pushing out
To scribble notes
Bubbles on the surface
She frightens easily
The nurse
Her hair tied up
Eyes big
And round
Afraid of heavy chairs
And minds
Invisible threats
How long have you been
Here?
Not
Stable enough to go home
Where the pain hides
And they won't
Talk
Out loud
Because it doesn't make sense

# We Are a Quilt: Discussion Questions

Use these questions to spark conversation about the poems, stories, and essays in this section.

## Medicine is the Best Medicine

by Alora Young

1. In this image, a young person's head is surrounded by medicine bottles. What do you think the photo is conveying? What emotional reaction does it evoke in you?

---

## Ode to My Antidepressants

by Alora Young

1. Medicine is the best medicine, is a line from this poem. How do you feel about people taking medication to treat a mental health condition? Do you wonder why they need to take medicine? Does it make you question their mental health more or less?

2. What do you think creates the stigma regarding mental illness and taking medicine for mental health?

3. Did this poem change your ideas or the way you feel about those who take medication for their mental health?

---

## Funny, In Hindsight

by Quan Williams

1. The narrator decided to tell us a story about how she was abused as a child from a more humorous perspective. How did that impact your perception of the abuse?

2. What does the reader learn about the mandated reporter and the social service system
that is supposed to protect the child?

3. From this brief account, we learn that abuse happened several times. Instead of taking the child away from the mother, should attending long-term counseling and mental health monitoring be a requirement for the child to stay in the home?

4. How do you think the parent feels about the story? Should it matter?

---

## Obsessive Compulsive Personality Disorder
by Akilah Brown

1. The author makes an interesting comment about criticism and abuse. "Living with a highly critical parent is a particularly insidious form of abuse because, for me, I can see how the criticism was supposed to help. It's hard, even still, to use the word abusive to describe the way I grew up." What do you think about criticism being viewed as a form of abuse? Do you think the parents understood what they were doing?

---

## Panic Attack: On the Edge of Oblivion by Angelique DeVonish, Underneath it All by Dana I. Hunter, Neurotic Animation by Mervyn Seivwright, Being Bipolar by Jasmine Vallejo-Love, Schizophrenia, anyone? By Lydia Theon Ware i, and Wading by Dana I. Hunter:

1. In each of these poems, the poets describe various symptoms. Do you think they offer a good glimpse into what the person suffering from mental illness might be experiencing?

2. Did their situations, descriptions, and/or comments that provide a new understanding or insight?

---

## Response Time
by Matthew E. Henry

1. Healthy Heritage Movement, Broken Crayons Still Color provided a course on Black mental health, where it was suggested that people should have an annual mental health checkup, the same way we have a physical health checkup. The poet may advocate the same thing as he asks about time travel. What do you think of the idea of getting an annual mental health checkup?

---

## Hoarder's Quilt
by Lydia Theon Ware i

1. The speaker in this poem poses a poignant question about mental illness and memory. What memories do you try to hold onto? Do you try to discard the messy, sorrowful memories from symptoms, things the sufferer of the illness may have done? Do you sanitize the memories?

---

## Light Switch by Beverly George, Sounds of Broken Glass by Brittany Miles, and A Letter to My Cousin by April Gardner:

1. In these four works, the speakers love someone with a mental illness. You can see the empathy and patience they have. What are some of the things that are cherished that offer hope? What advice would you have for them?

---

## Comfort
by Alora Young

1. In the photo titled "Comfort" by Alora Young, we see a young girl holding a stuffed animal and a bottle of medicine. Let's explore personal opinions and beliefs. Do you have an opinion on whether children should take medication for mental health conditions? What has influenced your opinion?

---

## The intrusive self-awareness posed by a long day of avoiding responsibilities in a fruitless attempt to ward off the pressing urge to simply give up, lie down, and cry
by Alora Young

1. In this poem, the speaker highlights things she is grateful for. What are they?

2. She also mentions some major irritants that she finds devastating. What are they?

3. Then there is the final feeling that leads her to a place of much needed rest and restoration. The reader is allowed to see the struggle, despite taking medication as prescribed as referenced in *Ode to My Anti-Depressants*. What insights do we gain about persistence, resilience, dedication and balance?

---

## Cracked
by Alexander James

1. In this new twist on an old nursery rhyme, HD has some very real-life stressors he is trying to manage. How is he finding meaning in his life? What are his fears?

2. Sometimes it is not what is said, but what is not said. Do you think there is a way HD might have come to a different conclusion?

## on monday, poet's head sang and hurt

by Jordan E. Franklin

1. The duplex is a literary form, a variation of the sonnet. Discuss the repetition of images and phrases in the poem and the overall tone and impact it has in allowing us to comprehend her emotional state.

---

## Seventy-two Hours

by Ginger M. Galloway

1. What is happening in this poem?
2. What are the points of frustration?
3. Does this seem like an overworked, short-staffed facility?
4. Do you think this is indicative of the mental health care facilities?

---

# Cutting-Nonsuicidal self-injury (NSSI)

Cutting, carving the skin, scratching, burning, or punching to cause self-pain, including embedding objects under the skin is NSSI. Self-injury is not the same as suicide. One is going to great lengths to stay alive. There is a high correlation between people who engage in self-injury, suicidal ideation and attempts. The behavior typically begins in early adolescence, between the ages of 11 and 14, and often decreases by early adulthood.

- NSSI experts state there is not a one-size-fits-all recovery plan. People with lived experience have found it beneficial to try out different techniques throughout their self-injury recovery journey.

# What are some safe alternatives?

- **Create a call list.** Write a list of confidants who you can call when urges arise. Be sure to ask them if they are comfortable being added to your call log.
- **Create a playlist.** Listen to your dedicated playlist when urges arise.
- **Crafting.** Keep your hands busy. Puzzles, painting, play doh, fidget toys have been helpful for people when trying to decrease urges.
- **Time yourself.** See if you can go 5 minutes, for example, without engaging in self-injury. Try to keep increasing the amount of time. The purpose of this exercise is to show yourself that you can refrain from self-injury for an allocated amount of time you set for yourself. Build your confidence, you got this!
- **Take a shower.**
- **Make a list** (on your phone or paper) **of small steps you can take to regulate.** Example: 1. Drink water. 2. Meditate. 3. Take a shower. 4. Eat something. 5. Watch a show/movie that makes you happy.
- **Emotional Freedom Technique** (EFT, Tapping).
- What to do when you feel like you are **struggling with NSSI - Text SH to 741741**
- Calm Harm is a free app that helps you manage or resist the urge to self-harm.

Source: Crisis Test Line. Free Support for Self-Injury. (2024, March 1). Retrieved April 26, 2026 https://www.selfinjury.bctr.cornell.edu/about-self-injury.html

# Voice for the Voiceless

If there are enough voices,
a cacophony of voices,
saying mental health care
is important in our communities,
you need to pay attention to this,
I think people don't have a choice
but to focus on it.

—Dr. Breland-Noble

# Mr. Somebody

by Chris TPG Green

He breaks out in hives during drives to the hospital.
The VA in VA keeps messing up his appointments
and he couldn't be more relieved.

Hospital floors are his horror film set of memories played.

Unwilling actor, he puts on a show whenever he signs in.
Remembers not being able to read to consent to the experiments.
Experiences episodes when he sees a lab coat.
Body still keeps the score.

Thought he was getting treatment for bad blood,
instead, medication withheld.
Daughter finds relief; he can no longer see where they're headed.

He needs a doctor,
says she's trying to keep him out the physical hands of God.
A new hospital still will see him as numbers,
but hopes she hits the lotto.

Her job got some healthcare.

A new president got her trembling; it won't be safe long enough.
Mr. Somebody on a time clock either way.

Wants to go out with some dignity.

Get away from the flashbacks.
Wants to die a man,
in a bed,

with socks on.

# Aftermath

by Devin Mitchell

Dead heat of August,
heavy traffic on Foothill
by the side of a mini mart,
not too far from a bus stop,

I watch the vet build his house
out of tree branches and dirty sheets
pulled from a dumpster.
He smells like rotting meat

and mint toothpaste. He brushes
his yellow teeth with an old brush,
grey with dirt spots on the handle
And only a few bristles.

Bathed in sweat, he covers his oily face
with a camouflage shirt,
almost hiding the scars on his neck
from the many failed hangings.

Old Black vet with an amputated leg
lost to IED shrapnel in the Gulf War
chirps his story at birds
as he feeds them bread.

During a tour in Kuwait,
he befriended a ring-necked parakeet
to talk to about comrades
paralyzed in fear – shot - blown up.

His guard dog is a pit-bull,
white with black spots, named "Bone."
People feed him scraps sometimes
when the vet is not home.

His wallet is a cup he waves at passersby.
When his cup is full, he buys
water, gas station hotdogs, dog food
sometimes toothpaste and bread.
After leaving the market

I hand him a new toothbrush,
a sandwich, water, and change.
I call him Sarge.

*Best time in my life. 'til it wasn't.*
*Ain't gonna complain. could be worse.*
*Soldiers always gotta be ready,*

*even if we got no country to care.*
*Thankful for those who do.*
He looks me in the eyes.

*Ring-necked parakeets are in the parrot family. They are imported birds found in Kuwait. Parrots are often used in therapeutic programs for veterans with PTSD because they are intelligent and empathetic creatures.

According to the Veterans Administration, in 2024, an estimated 32,882 vets were unhoused, and Black veterans account for a third of the homeless vet population.

# The Birthing Chamber

by Angela M. Franklin

You could hear her screams
subhuman worse than a black bear
caught in a steel trap
recalled an ear witness
to eyewitness news.

An abandoned Black woman pregnant,
bipolar-schizophrenic tethered
to a jail bed was in labor.

See, this is how they treat us.

The ear witness told story with back to camera
said never again ever would she want
to see what she saw and hear what she heard
the day a prisoner gave birth alone.

They thought Tammy was oblivious to pain
after her addiction to self-medicating cocaine,
the howling patient shunned and shamed.
Guards insisted Crazy Black women don't feel pain.

See, this is how they did her.

The woman's womb broke open.
Old caesarean keloids stretched and wept
labor's cruel tentacles pierced and pinched.
Help! she shouted, pushed and squatted 7 hours:

*Baby coming. Baby coming now. God, it hurts.*
*It hurts, please, please, please, somebody, please help me*
*Uh, uh, uuuhhh, oh God, it's coming, help us,*
*please, somebody have mercy, please, help me, oh Jesus!*

Sympathy pains punctured nearby vaginas
inmates in cells recalled their own birth agony,
wept with Tammy, screamed for help but jailers played
sadistic Dana I. Hunter with mother and fetus's health.
See, this is how they did them.

The blood-splattered birth chamber
resembled remnants of a Santeria ceremony
in the Divided States of America
a nation quilted in hatred
where even a dog gets more mercy.

Miranda fell from her mother
hit the floor and wailed, with palsied arms
Tammy cradled her bloody, mucous-covered baby
and whispered: *Mommy is so sorry.*

(Inspired by an article WPLG Local10.com, May 8, 2019)
The Birthing Chamber previously published in Peregrine, Volume XXXV, Black Poets Speak.

# mouthed silence

by Ginger M. Galloway

flesh torn into gaping little mouths
saying things that haven't been said
screaming hurts without tongue
understanding the cries
and not understanding
trying to catch red spittle
into white towel
the release must happen today
eyes wide with desperation
only you can help me,
but you won't
will you?
the salve won't hurt
from ungloved fingertip
into mouths
already pulling themselves shut
refusing to listen to lies
that paint the surface of walls
that cry in harmony
storybook pages written
in tiny lines
to tell as bedtime stories

# Mask Wearing a Mask:

Artist, Angela M. Franklin

# Peekin' [*Ready, let go*]
by Velvet Gunn

*Peekin' is a gripping tale about a young woman struggling to move forward after a devastating loss. The story delves into the complexities of family, the weight of grief, and the indomitable human spirit. Set in a house with Great Aunt Jean and younger sister Tamyra, Cameron fights to find redemption, solace, and normalcy within her new realities.*

SET
Vintage "kitchen" with open window externally covered in vines. Peeking through, you'll see a small round kitchen table with three chairs.

CHARACTERS

**Cameron Bell Jeffrey** - Eldest Sister, 24, attractive. A young chef in the making, who believes she'll one day be a great wife to her husband, once she gathers the importance of cleaning. She loves her family and wants nothing but to protect those she loves.

**Tamra "Tam" Bell** - Younger Sister, 12, dark short hair, spunky, comical. Tamra loves her Doll Dolly and enjoys sneakin' to watch messy talk shows at night.

**Buckley** – Brother to Tamra and Cameron.

**Jean Bell** - Great Aunt, early-50s, gray and brown hair, tall, a proud aunt who adopted three of her sister's children after she went missing. She feels her life has more purpose with having taken Tam, Cameron, and Buckley in.
**Darren Jeffrey** - Fiancé of Cameron, 27, a factory worker, only child, smitten over Cameron. He would do anything for her and their family.

**Officer 1**

**Officer 2**

---

**ACT I**

[ Ext. rain & thunder sounds]
[Int. kitchen]

*Cameron enters the stage SL to walk into the kitchen. She grabs a glass and pours herself some lemonade from a pitcher. She then sets the pitcher on the counter/table and then goes to sit by the window, looking out at the audience.*

**Cameron:** *[Taking a few sips, listening to the thunder and watching the water outside the window]* Have you ever been present? Like, for sure that you're here? Recognizing the colors that you see and the spirits that you feel? - Have you ever been like [*exhale and giggle*] without a care in the world about what you have to do when ya get home or 'bout things that disturb ya? ooor wonderings, just about money - Have you ever been present?

**Jean:** [*shouting*] Cameron?!

**Cameron:** Yeeees!

**Jean:** Set that table in there, will ya?

**Cameron:** [*sarcastically*] Why not?!

**Jean:** Pardon?!

**Cameron:** [snickering] Yes, Ma'am.
*Cameron jumps down from the chair at the window, starts removing old plates from the table, and washes dishes. As a sign of relief, Cameron gently places her open palms flat on top of the table. Tam then enters, talking to her doll and sits in the DL chair with legs crisscross applesauce, brushing her doll's hair.*

*Finally noticing Tamra, Cameron sneaks over to snatch Tamra's doll from up over her head, but Tamra catches it in time - then sashays over towards the window, looking back at Cameron. Tam sticks out her tongue and sits on the stool by the window. Both she and the doll are in the audience's view.*

**Tamra:** [*talking to her doll and the audience*] Here we are, you and me. You know I could be doing sum'n better than sitting here lookin' at your ugly face, but here we are again - Them cloudy skies, the rain, and you - lookin' like ugly.

**Cameron:** [*sweeping the floor*] You know if both y'all wasn't so ugly, your brain might work to alert you of the most cautionary actions you MIGHT take in gettin' down off that stool and helpin' me in this kitchen.

**Tamra:** [*side eyeing Cameron, fixing her doll's clothes*] I ain't helpin' you with nothing. Sharp teeth like that, you might-a considered using em' as a secondary set of hands to help ya gon' finish up. See we lookin' for excitement! Something a woman needs in her life to keep livin' and be strong. I ain't thinkin' bout cleaning up when you're here. That excitement, I left just for you.

*Jean is walking in, stage left.*

**Jean:** Alright now...

*Cameron and Tamra both stick their tongues out at each other again. Tamra hops down from the stool and runs over to give her a kiss on the cheek. Jean walks to the other side of Cameron leans over to give her a kiss on the cheek as well. Tamra then grabs a pitcher of lemonade and pours it into the glasses. Jean sits, and then Tamra. Cameron goes off stage and brings back a bowl, stirring it, and then serves a warm stuffed roll to each of them on a plate.*

**Jean:** You treat me well, Cameron. I'm shol' gon' miss ya when I'm gone. All this good cooking this week. [ *Looking over her shoulder out the window*] I was hoping your brother would be home by now, but we'll just save em' sum'n.
*Cameron places a bowl and spoon in the middle of the table and takes a seat.*

**Cameron:** [*scooting up to the table*] Now hold up, Aunt Jean... Don't start talking like that. You ain't leavin' me again, and I ain't leavin' you. Last month, I sat in a lady's hair chair for 75 minutes, and that's about as long as I ever wanna be away from you again.

**Jean:** [*laughing*] Mm-Hm

**Tamra:** He ain't comin'. He never come. You'd think for such an occasion, he would wanna be here, but he ain't comin'. [getting louder] Not now, not next month, not ever —

[*Tamra jumps up to run off stage, but stops at Aunt Jean's voice*]

**Jean:** I beg your pardon, little girl. You should be grateful and forever honorable to the sacrifices your brother has made for this family!

**Cameron:** [*leans over to touch Tamra's hand*] I'm just grateful that you all could be here. To share this time with me - and for however long we got together, I wanna make it special. I'm sure Buckley's just handlin' some business and wishes he was here too.

**Jean:** You know, before I took y'all in, I didn't have much purpose. My life was just a lot of seasons, and no nothin'. I'm grateful that I have ya, but if YOU [pointing to Tamra] don't settle that mouth of yours, Ima be grateful to put ya out. *Tamra tries not to laugh, but flops back down in her chair. Cameron winks at her and they stretch out their hands out to pray.*

**Jean:** Bow your heads. Lord, we wanna thank you for bringing us together again for another beautiful meal prepared by our own Chef Cameron - to feed our stomachs, our hearts, and our souls.

**Everyone:** Amen
*Starting to eat, they pass around the pepper at the table.*

**Cameron:** So, Ms. Tam, what's been showing on the television lately?

**Tam:** [*gesturing Cameron to be quiet*] Television? We don't watch no television. Especially not at night.

**Cameron:** [*laughing and eating*] I didn't say nun' bought the night. You stay tellin' on yourself smarty pants.

*Cameron suddenly starts gagging, covers her mouth, and runs off stage.*

**Tam:** Must be all that pepper she put on that tuna roll. Ooor she been screw-

**Jean:** Hush ya mouth Miss Tam ...

*Cameron comes back in. They both watch her as she sits back down. Wiping her mouth, she guzzles the lemonade and belches.*

**Jean:** Well, now...

*Cameron, smiling and a bit jittery.*

**Jean:** [*smiling*] Here we are to celebrate your engagement and look as if we 'bout to celebrate somethin' else too.

**Cameron:** Look like it ...

**Jean:** Least you a married woman.

**Tamra:** Almost a married woman.

**Jean:** [*side eyeing Tamra*] You know you girls can't hide nothin' from me - Had a dream just last week 'bout fish and you the only chicken I really know around these parts with some fresh eggs. — And I know it wadn't you, suga — [*Pointing to Tam*] By the way, I know you been watching them shows when I'm 'sleep. Walking 'round here reciting quotes and testaments about a womanhood and life you have YET to know ANYTHING about!

[*turning back to Cameron*]

**Cameron:** I'm excited, Aunt Jean. I know I ain't married yet, but I'm on the way. [*looking at Tam*] I imagine she'll look just like you, Tam.

**Tam:** *[smiling]* Then I know she'll be gorgeous.

*They all snicker and go back to eating.*

**Jean:** What time will Darren be here today to pick ya up?

**Cameron:** Well, he kinda dunno I'm here.

**Jean:** Of course he does.

**Cameron:** Naw, I was s'pposed to be at some meetin' - talk to some folks, and relax, they say.

**Tam:** And you chose to come back here?! That was stupid!

**Jean:** Somethin' I dunno is that man loves ya. A lot of times, people won't stick around. In good or bad times - and I've seen 'em stick around in both. Do good by him. Yall-a soon be raisin' a family of your own, and there you'll find your own purpose, but only love gonna drive it and keep it warm - keep it livin'. I got a bit of news too. You're lookin' at somebody who may be getting a new stove in these here comin' weeks.

**Tam:** Ya mean Cam's gonna have an opportunity to cook more of these mystery meals?!

**Cameron:** The real mystery, Miss Tamra, is how my next pie will have Dolly in it.

**Tamra:** [stands up and hits the table] Blasphemin'!

**Jean:** Sit down, Tamra!

**Tamra:** Sorry ...

**Cameron:** [*looking into the sky*] I got plenty of meals in mind! Roasted Chicken and Red Rue veggies. Duck and gravy with wheat and rice. Brussels and Smothered Beef Necks.

**Jean:** I can taste it now!

**Tam:** You really gon' be fat then.

*Cameron reaches over towards Tam and rubs her hair wildly.*

**Cameron:** *[Talking to Tam]* Hey, maybe it be a little girl you can play dolls with. Do her hair - show her how to fluff her socks like you like.

**Tam:** [*smiling*] That-a be nice.

Suddenly, a loud knocking comes from the door.

[*intense music begins*]

*Aunt Jean & Tam look at Cameron. Cameron looks forward, eyes bucked, hands flat on the table, and heavy breathing. Cameron then looks to Tam and Aunt Jean. Both Jean & Tam rise up from their chairs, with their eyes still on Cameron, but nothing is said. Pushing in their chairs, they both slowly walk away to opposite sides, off stage.*

*[spotlight and faded lights if feasible]*

*The knock gets louder, and Cameron jumps up to start clearing the table and room as it originally was. In the midst of her cleaning, she begins reciting a monologue.*

**Cameron:** [*Talking to herself and the audience*] Much as I wanna cry my heart out right now — I can't. Much as I wanna pour into the people around me and let them know everything I'm feeling, I can't. Wouldn't be necessary, as this time tears won't suffice, and my words just fall on deaf ears. They say I'll have to do something different this time, and as much as I hope and dream that my friends and family gon' always be there — they won't. They're unable to, and here I am with shoes too big and awkward to make any sense. Too dirty to be cleaned, cuz I shoulda checked the stove, I shoulda checked it when I —

*A LOUD THUMP rings in the room as police Officers bust through the door, chasing Cameron around the table and then pins her to the floor. One officer gets up and goes off stage to "scan the house."*

**Officer 1:** Mrs. Jeffery, now I hate to have to keep visiting with you like this, but you seem to be in some danger to yourself and those around you.

**Cameron:** No danger here Officer - Just makin' lunch for me and my gals.
The other officer returns.

**Officer 2:** What gals she talkin' 'bout? I don' checked the house. Nobody here.

**Officer 1:** Puts his head down in disbelief, looks up, and nods in agreement with the other officer. Picking Cameron up, he sits her in a chair at the table [*Aunt Jean's seat*]. [*Walking over to the window, Officer 1 peeks out while Officer 2 stands by and watches Cameron*].

**Officer 2:** So what we gon' do with her?

**Officer 1:** [*chuckling*] Much as she breaks in this place, I'd put her back in the loony house, but by her Husband's order, we wait for 'im to get here so he can take — her home.

**Officer 2:** .... And what about the house? Breaking and entering? Vandalism? Trespassing?

[*Officer walks over toward Cameron. Circling her a bit.*]

**Officer 1:** [Chuckling again] Technically, it's her house. Lady named Jean Bell left it to her in a will before she passed away two years ago.

**Cameron:** That lady was my aunt, and you should let me go since you know so much. It is MY house!

**Officer 1:** - Let you go? She should-na let you in here to begin with.
Cameron attempts to get up, but Officer 2 pushes her back in her seat.

**Officer 1:** Six years ago, Ms. Bell, [*angrily*] who was a close friend of mine, adopted her sister's three kids after she don' ran off. [*exhale*] As I'm told, Jean call herself runnin' to the store - left Miss thing here to watch out for the house [*pointing to Cameron*] but wadn't no good cuz she set a fire!

**Cameron:** I ain't did no sucha thing! [*Cameron goes into a daze and exhales*] Blueberry muffins, fresh eggs, blood orange juice, and sliced pork. [*She opens her hands flat on her lap with palms open*] 6:45 AM I walked to the back to play with the chickens, and I just for sure knew the time it would take to be finished cookin'. Left a cloth on the stove. [*Goes back to talk about the chickens*] They runnin' and runnin' and I'm laughin' at em'. Aunt Jean waved to me—let me know she was back — and then all I heard was Buckley screaming [*voice doubled with Cameron's - Buckley - AUNT Jean!!! TAAAAM !!!!*]

**Cameron:** And then he called my name, but before I could realize he wasn't callin' to be funny — it was too late. Them chickens stopped laughing, and my heart started pounding, cuz all you could see was smoke - Tried to touch the door, the winda (window) - I just went peekin', and there it was - wadn't no more Tam, wadn't no more Aunt Jean. Wadn't no more Buckley.

The officers look at each other. Suddenly, there's a knock on the door. Once Cameron realizes who it is, she starts to hyperventilate.

**Cameron:** Darren !!!!

*Cameron attempts to run towards him, but Officer 2 pulls her back down to her seat by her restraints. Darren storms towards the Officer, but Officer 1 holds him back and gives a head gesture for Officer 2 to let her go, and heads towards the front door. Darren pierces her with his eyes as she walks out. Once both Officers leave the room, Darren and Cameron embrace like it's been centuries.*

**Cameron:** [*apologetic*] - D... I -

**Darren:** Shhh. I already know, and ain't no need of ya worryin' ya-self by explaining.

**Darren:** Did they hurt you?

**Cameron:** Not physically. That black officer made me feel like I was a murderer, the devil himself.

**Darren:** But we know that's not true.

**Cameron:** I told 'em how I felt, though. Told my side of the story — and it still hurt — but I remember the day when things were hard to say - but now I want, and I need to be myself ya know - and if they don't like it, I frankly don't care - I'm sorry I ran away again, Darren. I just had to see 'em. [*looking over to Darren*] But what about you? [*head down*] What about me?

*Darren takes Cameron by both hands and brings her closer.*

**Darren:** About you, you gon' be alright. We gon gon' see that Doctor about that other elixir for you. Whatever we gotta do to keep you home. As for me [*placing his hand on her face*], I'm just happy to be with ya, Cammy. With my whole bein'. I missed you. [*They both smile at each other*].

**Cameron:** I missed you, too.

**Darren:** Did you see 'em today?

**Cameron:** Yeah

**Darren:** Was it a good visit?

**Cameron:** Yea ...

**Darren:** Did Buckley come this time?

**Cameron:** Tam put a glass out for em' — thought he would show, but he didn't.

**Darren:** [*smiling but looking down*] Cammy .... I don't really know how to say this to you, but the Judge ordered the house to be sold. [*Cameron looks shocked and upset. She grabs a bag and starts filling it with items in the house (bag prefilled off stage)*] Judge say it's cause of your condition [*inhale and rephrases his statement*] because of your state of mind. [*Cameron then goes over to the window. Darren is about to follow her, but she holds her hand out for him to wait*].

**Darren:** [*Standing up with his hands in his pockets.*] I'm sorry, baby. I promise to make new memories for ya and make plenty space for you to cook them big dinners. We can start havin' more folks over. Doc says it be good for you too.

*Cameron goes off into a daze.*

**Cameron:** I knew something was going on. Aunt Jean was just about to buy a new stove.

**Darren:** I'll get you a new stove, honey. Whatever you like .... Now let's get out of here for they come back and drag us out.

**Cameron:** I can't leave 'em like this Darren. Them folks ain't gonna know what to do for Aunt Jean or be able to take Tam's attitude.

*Darren gets up and walks DL with his hands in his pockets.*

**Darren:** [*trying not to yell*] THEY - They, gonna try and take you away from me, Cammy [*looks over his right shoulder*]. Baby please. I can take care of you. I know they need you, but I need you more. Life be for the livin', and I don't wanna spend another night without you with me. Please....

**Cameron:** Cameron comes from the window and puts her hands on his shoulders. He turns to her, and they embrace each other. I know it's time to let go, but I ain't go never let go.

**Darren:** [*lifting up her chin*] And you don't have to. You can keep em' right here [*gently taps her chest*] You have to forgive yourself, Cammy. You have to give yourself permission to live again and reimagine life - without the guilt, without the worry, without havin' to fix it. God knows and so do they, but now it's time for you to know. Cameron lets out a long sigh.

**Cameron:** [*snatching away from him and walking DR*] Fine - but I'll only go home with you if [*pauses*] we can start working on a nursery too.

**Darren:** Nursery? [*Darren runs to kneel down in front of her and puts his head on her belly*] Charon, Carren, and Darren Jr., are you in there?

**Cameron:** Oh, you expectin' three babies, are ya?

**Darren:** And plenty more, Mrs. Jeffrey [*Darren stands up, brings her DC, and spins her around*] Wish Aunt Jean coulda known it. She'd spoil em' all rotten.

*Cameron smiles and wipes the tears from her eyes.*

**Cameron:** [*Grabbing hold of Darren's hand*] She knows .... Ready? Let's go.

*Music starts to play as the lights fade, and they walk offstage.*

*Black Out with music still playing slightly in the background.*

– The end.

# Jane

by Sharon M. Williams

There's a woman named Jane
who sleeps where shadows gather.
Her belongings are her pillows—
a pocketknife, a scrap of peace.

Above her, the overpass howls
with cars that once carried her to work.
Her mind is a thicket of voices.
Her feet, once pedicured,
are caked with the city's dust.

Strangers pass with quick movements,
dimmed eyes, faces closed like locked doors.
They tune out her sermons
about the rapture,
about grace.

Still, she speaks hope
into a world that has forgotten how to listen.
Her brown legs wrapped in trash bags,
her hair tangled like memory.

She is a universe of love
trapped inside a system
that does not know how to hold her.
She still sees her high heels,
still sees her baby,
the one she lost
before the world lost her.

Tremors move beneath her skin,
unseen.
By the time they surface,
something inside
has already broken.

She sits for hours,
quiet,
stitching together her soul.
Threading dignity

through every torn seam.
Trying to become
whole again.

She looks up at the sky
and continues stitching.
Not for rescue—
but for herself.

# A Letter to My Cousin

by April Gardner

Dear Cousin,

Fashionista runway model, Different World diva, thank you for the Lee Press on Nails at the age of five, and the pink Barbie lipstick, which my mother did not approve of. Thank you for your efforts to teach me how to act and look like a little girl. I say thank you because if it were not for those gifts, I would never have come to the conclusion that being girlie is not for me.

Instead of the gifts geared towards my gender, I appreciated your moments of candor. On the days when you decided to take your medication and were talking your truth, thank you. And on the days when your voices were not too loud, I heard you. I remember secrets you shared about famous folks who tried to hide who they are, fooling everyone and no one at the same time.

Your life as a model was as unconventional as a model could be. Two percent of the time you took your medication, and in the ninety-eight percent of the time where you refused, I learned what true rage looks like as the voice in your heart and head. I could be ten feet away from you and feel your seething fury.

From birth to fifteen, we were friends. In one year, you aged ten. You were running in circles, chased by invisible monsters we couldn't see. When rage swallowed you whole, I said goodbye. When your spirit was no longer here, you were able to hear me again; my words were tears. The word goodbye was already spoken. So I now say what I meant to say a long time ago,

I miss you.

# 2000 Episodes

by Angela M. Franklin

on a good day my brother hallucinated

believed he could speak Tagalog
to pick up mail-order Filipinas

but
it
was
nonsense

our untrained ears heard his words a cacophony of bee hives, crows, chicken cluck sounds

erupt unseen through his chest exit throttled throat

his words accelerated thudded like a drug-rushed parachute

brain could not keep up

he bobbed /weaved/ danced in red rubber soled Kungfu shoes/ belted ghee/shaved
head/ studied Bruce Lee/sketched women lizard-like / half human/ half beast/ hosted
broken angels/tasted their sweat/swore he was clean/but wasn't/eyes bloody moons/
hustled us/ hustled himself broke/collected new friends/on general relief payday/
broke same day/

our sibling

never violent never violent never violent
depression poured through his pores
meth mix offered a temporary fix for loneliness

forty years of agony finally freed in dirty green ocean water off California coast

# Reflections of a Smoke Detector

by Angela M. Franklin

Bipolar battered my brother's brain senseless.
He ditched his room, pitched a tent on Skid Row
after voices advised, *Kill the government's eyes.*
I saw psychosis slither thick inside his dark temples.

He ditched his room, pitched a tent on Skid Row
after smoke detector screamed at fridge
psychosis snaked thick trails in brother's brain cells.
His bedroom curtains watched, shook in fear.

After smoke detector screamed at fridge
itchy voices cried, *Destroy the ceiling spies*!
Bedroom curtains shook in fear
when brother crushed his pink pills.

Itchy voices cried, *Destroy sneaky ceiling spies.*
They hitched a ride inside his Target shopping cart,
after he stomped his pink pills.
Baby brother obeyed Nestor, an unholy ghost of a friend.

For thirty-nine years, I saw psychosis slither thick in Mark's temples,
after Nestor, his pretend childhood friend, gave useless solutions
to a bipolar brain battered senseless
who said *Go make a bed of concrete*, and he listened.

# When Grief Takes a Turn for the Worse

by Angela M. Franklin

I.

Call me, touched. But when Roz enshrined some of her beloved Angelo's ashes inside a silver, heart-shaped pendant and matching ring, I recoiled thinking of the once-strapping, 6' man now housed in 1 ½ inches of space resting on her finger and neck. She felt at peace with particles of her lover. When she visits, I wonder *which part of him* lies inside her jewelry– his arm, leg, or eye.

II.

I bristled. Roz's obsessive devotion gave me the willies. Thoughts of burnt flesh and bone fragments rattled mine--until the time I picked up my beloved brother's gray, powdery remains poured and sealed inside a clear, vinyl bag, housed in a thin, black, plastic box. I *mused is that all there is of him*--all 5'8" of Mark's once lithe, muscular body now granular calcium.

III.

He collapsed in the gutter. They found him unconscious near Smart and Final. Thirteen years of Skid Row living culminated like nine hundred other lives that year. For four hundred eighty months, Mark wrestled wicked twins bipolar and schizophrenia. He'd protest *I can't live in no dirty motel. They are filthy and have bed bugs. His last words to me. But you're lying on pissy, spit-stained sidewalks!* I shouted. What did I understand about his sidewalk liberty—freedom of sleeping undisturbed. Until one cold LA morning, street cleaners found him nearly frozen to death by the elements. No frost or snow necessary. I heard meth users feel hot, unaffected by cold temperatures.

IV.

We tried for years to resurrect the brother we once knew. I placed the one-and-a-half-pound container of him on my coffee table for his memorial services. After an hour, I sensed he wasn't comfortable there. I moved him to the fireplace mantel. He didn't like it there either. On to the bookshelf he went, where he scoffed, leaving me unsettled. No matter where I placed his remains, I couldn't sleep. A few days later, when we lowered the basket of flowers and his ashes into the Pacific Ocean, he and I could finally rest.

# Voice for the Voiceless: Discussion Questions

Use these questions to spark conversation about the poems, stories, and essays in this section.

## Mr. Somebody

by Chris TPG Green

1. The veteran in this poem has had traumatic experiences that leave him angry and untrusting. What events has the government perpetrated against him as a Black man? How does this impact his behavior when he goes to the VA? How has the government's betrayal impacted the vet's mental health (diagnosis/misdiagnosis)?

2. What does his daughter want for him, and what does he want for himself?

---

## Aftermath

by Devin Mitchell

1. What does the vet in this poem suffer from? Why is he homeless? It appears the government has failed to provide this vet with proper care. How does this happen?

---

## The Birthing Chamber

by Angela M. Franklin

1. Who is Tammy? What is her mental illness diagnosis? Where is she as she has her baby? What does the description of the birthing sound like?

2. Are you surprised this happened in 2019? How might it evoke scenes and the horrors of slavery? Why does Tammy apologize to Miranda?

3. Do you think things have changed since 2019? What do you think we can do to create change for pregnant women in prison?

## mouthed silence

by Ginger M. Galloway

1. If the wounds from someone cutting could speak, what do you think they would say?

2. Within the Black community, self-harm is sometimes hidden or ignored due to stigma. If you notice someone is self-harming, what actions do you think you could take as a friend or family member?

3. Why do you think a person would resort to cutting?

---

## Mask Wearing a Mask

by Angela M. Franklin

1. In Paul Laurence Dunbar's famous poem "We Wear the Mask," he describes the idea of wearing a mask. For a person with mental health symptoms, it is often said that they wear a mask to hide their struggles and try to fit in. What might be some of the long-term effects of masking?

---

## Peekin' [Ready, let go]

by Velvet Gunn

1. Is a solution or remedy presented to help Cameron? How is the court system helping her? How is her family helping her? How is she helping herself, or can she help herself?

2. What more can be done?

## Jane
by Sharon M. Williams

1. There is an ever-increasing need for housing and for mental health facilities in our country. Jane is one of thousands of homeless women in the United States. She is not a menace or danger to herself or others. What options does she have?

---

## 2000 Episodes, Reflections of a Smoke Detector, and When Grief Takes a Turn for the Worse by
by Angela M. Franklin

1. These three poems are a brief glimpse into the life of the poet's brother. Knit together, they tell a devastating turn of events. Talk about the concrete images and details that allow the reader to understand Mark's illness and limited options.

2. Was there any way that he might have been helped by the mental health system?

3. Do you have suggestions for programs we currently have or could create?

# What to do when you feel like you are struggling.

Please reach out to 988 Lifeline

You can text, call or chat. 988 is a Lifeline. They are available 24/7. It's free, and confidential. There are counselors who will listen and support you without judgment. If you feel like you or someone you see or know is in physical danger, call 911 instead of 988.

**Black Teen Suicide Rate:** The suicide rate among Black adolescents is increasing faster than other racial and ethnic groups. From 2007 to 2020, the suicide rate rose 144% among 10 - to 17-year-olds who are Black. Although the overall youth suicide rate is trending downwards, this data raises alarms about the need to improve and address mental health care for Black communities.[1]

**Silent Pain Black Men and Depression:** Watch the Roland S. Martin Video: Justin Fairfax murder-suicide. The conversation centers on the reality that many Black men are conditioned to suppress pain, avoid vulnerability, and carry emotional burdens without support. Emotional suppression, lack of access to care, and cultural expectations around masculinity create a dangerous environment. **Without intervention, without spaces for Black men to process pain, and without confronting the stigma around mental health, the same cycle will continue.**[2]
*trigger warning for the video.

**Suicide Rates Among Black Women and Girls Have Climbed for Two Decades.** Increases in suicide in the United States over the last two decades have disproportionately affected Black young women. Rates were highest in the West, peaking at 4.8 per 100,000 among individuals 25–34 years, and deaths were concentrated in the South.[3]

**People often turn to suicide because they are seeking relief from pain. Please know we care and there are people who can help.**

1) Farzana Akkas and Allison Corr. (2024, April 22) "Black Adolescent Suicide Rate Reveals Urgent Need to Address Mental Health Barriers." Retrieved April 26, 2026, fromhttps://www.pew.org/en/research-and-analysis/articles/2024/04/22/black-adolescent-suicide-rate-reveals-urgent-need-to-address-mental-health-care-barriers
2) Video: Roland S. Martin: "Justin Fairfax murder-suicide. Black Male Psychologists break it down." (17. April 2026). Retrieved April 26, 2026. https://www.youtube.com/watch?v=tn_AqUCNNWg
3) "Suicide Rates Among Black Women and Girls Have Climbed for Two Decades" (6, December 2023) https://www.publichealth.columbia.edu/news/suicide-rates-among-black-women-girls-have-climbed-two-decades

# Internal Struggle to Live

It's challenging to talk about how you're doing mentally
since it's an invisible injury — people can't see it,
so it's harder to understand,
but I think that's why it's so important we feel empowered
to open up about it.

—Simone Biles

# One Hundred Minutes

by Brandon Allen

*Suicide is the second leading cause of death for adolescents ages 10-24 in the U.S. Every 100 minutes a teenager takes their own life. That's a little over fourteen kids a day.

1

I was never introduced to depression; it just took me hostage.
It forced me inmate ideations, would warden the halls of my juvenile mind.
I was twelve the first time I finally found the one thing that cut deeper than words.

2

It takes two hours to watch a Marvel movie.
At the same time, a ticking time bomb of a teen is starring in their final scene.
Curtains close, credits roll,
yet there's nothing left for you to see at the end of this show.
There's no return for the sequel.

3

I weigh over 300 pounds.
I'm not exactly somebody you wanna wrestle.
Matter of fact, imagine me sitting on your chest,
and trying to breathe.
Anxiety feels a lot like an allergic reaction to the thoughts in your head.
Anaphylactic shock triggered by something that was said.
Anxiety masquerades as mountains, cascading its shadow with every step.
I'm 6'3 and it still makes me feel short of breath.

4

For years depression was a cuss word in our culture.
Forced to cap the volcanoes of our emotions,
cover our natural fury pre-disaster,
like the plastic on our grandparents couches
we could all see through it,
yet it made them feel more comfortable
if you pretended it wasn't there.
Made cleaning messes simpler.

They just ignored the rumbling of our cores,
leaking lava that ran down our cheeks.
We, Vesuvius bursting at the seams,
becoming the only casualties of Pompeii
leaving nothing but ashes and poetry.

5
Your brain can only go without oxygen for five minutes before dying.
How many teens have been holding their breath in our vicinity,
and we never take notice?

Hang their anger and outrage in the closets we've forced them to call home,
then show up surprised with tears in our eyes, too late to resuscitate.

6
Depression isn't something you can just wash off,

7
or pray and pray and pray away.

8
Have you ever been mocked by your own demons,
wondering why you showed up to a war and brought the wrong weapons?

9
Their ideations aren't contagious,
it's okay to give them hugs, wipe their tears, and sit with them in their pain.

10
You just have to be willing to face your own.

11
Eleven-year-olds today have the agency
to fully talk about how they feel.
We just have to listen.

12
Midnight is the darkest hour
when depression has placed you in solitary confinement.

Isolation is death's best friend.

13
Let's not forget these numbers have doubled and tripled due to the pandemic.
Let's not forget that this pain is real.
Let's not forget this pain.
Let's not forget.

Fourteen kids die every day from suicide.

*Source: American Academy of Pediatrics, 2024

# Long as Memory

by Chris TPG Green

I remember him

The party traveled with him
Rode shotgun
Light bounced off his smirk it seemed
Visibly physically the strong friend
A headlock felt like thoughts could spill
A coach's dream of a football build

I remember him

Changing the tides of the day
Filling the hallway with laughter
Loud as the cheers from the rafters when he played

It was thunder wearing speakers

I felt my eardrums burst at the homecoming game
When he received his crown

I hope he received his crown

Looking back

I wonder how many signs were missed, too busy making ones to cheer for him
I can't help but wonder why it wasn't enough

Why, with so many of us surrounding him, did he still feel so alone?

I remember he could have a look like he saw a silver line
I remember the time his smile had no shine to it

I wonder

Do I have the strength to say enough is enough?
The strong friend telling himself

The outcome was better than figuring out how to save him
more burden than hero

I don't know
I will never have those answers, I just know

He will live long as my memory

# How Are You?

Artist: Davian Chester.

HOW ARE YOU? HONESTLY, I TRULY WANT TO KNOW..

# Break the Piñata on Timothy Street

by Mario Tahi Lathan

I whirled around for years,
Unlike New Testament Paul,
I was not a companion
                                        break the piñata on timothy street.
Even as Only Son indulged
In an army of Penny Candy recruits,
Having GEDs in Boston Baked Beans,
          Associates in Noun Later,
          Bachelors in Lemonheads,
          And Masters in the Tootsie Roll.
                                        Break the Piñata the Piñata
Boomerang traffic, I would trek on the sixty.
Piled high a backpack of Burnett silence, Bourdain dreams,
And eighties Oprah, first episode of "What Did Not Come to Be."
                                        BREAK the Piñata on... BREAK the Piñata
Skirmishes lead to sake-driven scenes,
Clashes, faked carnal love stand-ins.
With two DUIs, a neon-colored world
Littered by Pocket-Change-Girls on walls, sans emotional hue.
                                        BREAK the Piñata on Timothy Street.
My war raged as a scar of abandonment ensued.
Only Daughter revealed my wounds, a weakness,
Mistaken for kindness.          Break-Break-Break-Break
A ceasefire, birthed from Dyslexic smiles.
                                        The Piñata on Timothy Street.
The *politicians* canvas only the white fenced streets,
belting campaign promises to deprive
Father's-hood
Of Father's sanity.

Break the Piñata on Timothy Street.
A bitter chorus hummed by Bass soloists
                                        Break      the Piñata            on Timothy Street
placed front and center,
Breakthepiñataon timothystreet          Breakthepiñataon timothystreetBreak
                              A Muppet version of Jacob's Panel #15
Stopped
            by Black Jesus,
                              with a call
                              from Mother Beverly.

# I am a Romantasy Rewriting Herself

by Camille Hernandez

The pews of St. Irenaeus Catholic Church sigh in relief, knowing they no longer need to hold up the girl who prayed to die. They labored through hushed whispers of a girl stained in the stale scent of pristinely varnished yet undusted mahogany. Unclaimed mysteries tried to ignite the possibility that there's more to life than staying alive. The pews heard me and recalled the days it was once a tree – alive, rooted, and splayed in its glory – before it became the dead and beautiful thing used to hold up people who recite endless liturgies and romanticize life after death. There lies the irony of my childhood: I was the girl wishing for death while the dead thing I sat on was holding me in my darkest prayers.

From the age of ten to my late twenties, I begged in circles for my life to end. The violence of living overwhelmed me, and I wanted to be born into the eternal life of Christian imagination. It was told that heaven is a beautiful place filled with fattened baby cherubs, who are obviously breastfed by the teats of dead nuns or some other symbol of pure womanhood. Those precious little pale chunky cherubs were good and holy and painted on the rooftops of cathedrals so people could revel in the wholesomeness of their nudity. (European Christian art is so awkward sometimes.) I was lanky, dirty, wiry-haired, dark-skinned, and too curvaceous to be considered a child. I believed every stereotype about me before I ever gave myself that chance to know who I was.

If love existed in my life, it was fighting its way out in a vacuum of hate.

My most fervent prayer was to make this terrible fate of living scurry off faster than a kitten in the spotlight. No matter how much I wanted to stop living, I couldn't. Day in and day out, I woke up and was... here.

Or, instead, there.

I was there. Waking up there on the futon in a crowded living room. There, listening to my dad's blaring Motown music. There, placated into following the Black ancestral routine of deep cleaning the house on Saturday mornings. This game of cat and light was the routine of my life: wake up early on Sunday morning, go to church, pray for my life to end, and spend the rest of the week drowning in disappointment. On the seventh day, my dad cleaned the house because he didn't know how to clean my resolve. Living was a constant practice in powerlessness.

I was a plaything in the hands of a fate practiced in cruelty towards dark-skinned girls. Bigotry is a violent education, and cruelty is its favored point. I was a powerless girl who believed she'd grow into a scandalized woman. If no one in a child's vicinity can imagine their thriving, then the child grows into the shattered prophecies of these horrid standards. I wish I could say my childhood was filled with the ruthless defiance of a girl dedicated to living above her station. I wish I could say my childhood was spent wanting to live. I want to be the poster child of a Black girl overcoming. But that's not me. It's not even half of me.

To say that I greeted adversity with an unwillingness to live is a flat story. Every moment of every day was filled with adversity. Even the deceptively small moments were filled with the overwhelm of losing the internal negotiation to approve myself. This is how my obsession with imagining my suicide began: I was overwhelmed and didn't know how to escape.

Overwhelm is a heaviness that makes its home past the predictable boundaries of fear and anxiety. To be overwhelmed is to hold everything that scares and stresses you while having no tools to help you carry the load. My mind was exquisitely trained in creating the traps of the hatred society set for me. I knew the world in ultimatums and little else. Wanting to kill myself meant I wanted to be placid in my ongoing storm of a life. I wanted to be a picture-perfect image of a child sleeping peacefully. I wanted to be crystallized in the romantic agelessness of maidenhood. But can one be remembered as a sacrificial virgin if her hair is not blonde, her skin is not milky white, and her lips are not as thin as the cruel lines of judgment separating her from humanity?

What good is dying if I can't even trust the living to entomb me in the peace I longed for?

Suicide is the most terrible of all art forms because the message is painted in the very last exhale on what was once a living canvas. When it comes to the art of suicide, leaving notes behind like breadcrumbs is a choice. Some people choose not to do it for many reasons. I didn't want to leave a suicide note behind because there's no point in naming all my hurts in a society that regularly celebrates it. Suicide is society's mirror, not someone's narrative ending. This corruption of living in a country built on stolen land is so ego-driven, fast-paced, and horror-mongering that it regularly misses the plot.

I wanted to die, and Death denied my request every day. Aware that I was trapped in this mishap of living, I turned myself from a suicide artist to a seductive crooner. I was a girl helpless to the art of living and failing at the pursuit of death, and this childhood misfortune taught me how to serenade what so many fear. If God wasn't answering my prayers, then maybe Death could hear my love songs.

First, I learned to sing on scales. Musical scales and tenderness scales. Tenderness is not a monolith; it's a scale measured by the ways we were raised and the tastes we developed. Some parents who truly love their kids don't know how to be gentle with them. A mean word, a period of silent treatment, and a hard hit are the only love some caretakers can provide because, to them, it's better than what they got in their childhood. It saddens me that children are expected to justify their pain and coddle the wounds of the adults who took care of them. I learned how to sing to Death with generations of unresolved pain. I trained myself in adagios that begged. When I speak of begging, I have a particular reference for it:

Nighttime.

Rainfall.

Baggy outfits.

Musical harmonies good enough to make the wind cry.

Someone is wearing sunglasses when they don't need to.

Two stanzas, an emboldened, infectious chorus, and a bridge strong enough to carry you into emotional intelligence

I begged for Death to come as if I were a '90s R&B musician. Those artists were bastions of emotion who taught me (and a whole generation of impressionable youth with good taste in music) how to beg well enough to be heard. I twisted their songs into prayers for my own damnation. Life was too hard, and I didn't have enough language to express my inner struggle, nor did I have accessible resources to tend to my mental health. I used their words and mimicked their heartache. I sang those lyrics with the dedicated fervor to get what I wanted: the end of the road, giving my all, if only for one night. When you are desperate enough to gamble your voice into a listening silence, you are coerced into becoming a mudworker setting blocks for their tower to heaven. Many people want you alive enough to be exploited, but never living freely. How many of us have enough language in our souls to describe the amount of heartache it takes to believe that dust and stillness are the only ones willing to listen to you.

I am alive enough to share my reflections on what it meant to be a suicidal adolescent. That is a victory that has required me to complete many inventories of my memories' stockroom. Are you expecting me to tell you when I magically decided to stop dying and start living? I don't have an answer for that. There is no magical moment when I decided that living was better than crooning to Death. This isn't a testament to my commitment to living. I was very dedicated to torturing myself slowly ad nauseam. Ambitious. Every day of life was a baby step and a wobble. Living to tell the tale doesn't make me a success story. Painting my portrait as the poster child for unsuccessful suicide attempts would, once again, shatter the mirror that suicide holds up to society.

So, reader, don't miss the plot this time.

My capacity to answer the question of why people end their lives is a cup half full. The air filling the other half of the cup is filled with questioning why I choose to live. Measuring my inquiries according to this image shows that the metaphorical cup is filled to the brim with unanswered questions. What I can answer you at this moment is that I was a child infatuated with Death. Little did I know that every prayer to God to end my life was a courtship song sung at Death's window. Death heard me and answered back in its loving cruelties of shame, humiliation, and pain. There we were, in this maddening courtship. I was the one performing songs in the deepest night, serenading Death to love me. And Death did love me.

Death still loves me.

Those decades spent at my worst and lowest, I was powerful enough to transform Death from a foreboding word into an exquisite romance. Every day, something has tried to absolve me of my humanity. Every day, something has tried to kill me. Every single day, I have made Death my biggest fan as this country worships me in hatred, carceral punishment, and state-sanctioned violence. There was never a point in my story where I chose to live. Instead, there was the eviscerating realization that Death yearns for me.

I am a sucker for a good romance. It just so happens that I live in one that will last my lifespan. When I do succumb to Death's loving embrace, it will not be by accident. It will be because I decided that their plea was too good.

Have decades of suicidal ideation made me so delusional that I believe death is obsessed with me? Maybe. But these delusions gave me the ability to carve an excellent life for myself out of the rotting wood of a country dedicated to hating me.

I continue to be so loved by Death that I can hear sweet nothings in every criticism, threat, and dehumanizing action I receive. I have not died... yet. I still think about Death a lot. I think about what it means to die and what will come after it. I'm finally at the place where I can contemplate Death without desiring to die. And isn't that how hope operates: as the delusion that keeps us tethered to a stubbornness that keeps our hearts beating? Death is a jilted lover, but it is not my greatest romance. When Death meets my standards, I will love them back.

# Death Still Checks in on Me

*After Maya Williams*

by Matthew E. Henry

I miss You, appreciate when Your familiar face
stops by for a chat. I remember inviting You
to be my plus one at that party, having my coat
in hand before I suddenly decided to stay
in for the night. You never complained.

not sure I ever thanked You for the hours
upon hours within hours You sat beside—
a hand on my shoulder, a head on my chest—
listening to my inconsolable bitching, or
riding shotgun as my leaded soul accelerated
my focus-less swerving through Denver traffic.
You were always so calm, made me feel safe.

but there was the time You told me—had me
convinced—You'd called in our reservation
a year in advance, only to take my father
for a few minutes instead. an amuse-bouche
You said after returning him in new clothes.
a misunderstanding I've mostly forgiven.

it's getting late and I know You've got places
to be. swing by any time. if the door's locked
the key is where I've always hidden it. no need
to call ahead. friends are always welcome.

# Sum Up a Day Compiled of Single Steps

by Eric DeVaughnn

you ask why more than usual—the pestering breath
of want. you try to write your way out of a paper bag
(why bother?) you look for shadows to point you home

*there is a fearlessness when*
*death seems your own invention*
*your neck does not swivel*
*your eyes refuse to kiss colors*
*they once loved, focused on shutter&sluice*
*each foot shuffles independent of the other*

*but you make your way forward*

*rote repetition routine*
*rote repetition routine*

you contemplate the gradual stretch of shadows
fill a brown paper bag with reluctant breath. it shakes
free of your chest, to no ovation. you do not ask why

# ~~The Real Monster Is Never~~ Being Able to Place the Sound of

By Jordan Franklin

1. your breathing
2. cracks in the walls
3. the lines in your head
    a. open-ended
    ~~b. open-mouthed~~
4. your body ~~splintering~~
5. your blood
    a. arrhythmic epigenetics
    b. the veins' loud swelling
6. the ~~bitter~~ sweetness of your spit as
    ~~a. it fights your mouth~~
    ~~b. you lay between the jaws of this cold apartment~~
7. your mind ~~failing~~
8. the night split
    a. into a new act
    b. drags itself like sun
    c. down its beaten road of sky
9. more ~~breaking~~
10. all this ~~rage~~
    ~~a. turned inward~~
    ~~b. denying every ending~~
11. your box breaths on the pillow at dawn
12. another ~~unwanted~~ day as yourself
13. every part of you marveling at
    *a. how you are here*
    *b. how you lived ~~through all this noise~~*

# Suffocating Husk
by James Coats

Don't think about how you'll do it.
Don't lie on your bed at 3:00 a.m.
and replay all the mistakes.
How you zigged when you should have zagged.
Don't think about the mounting debt,
small paycheck, growing exhaustion,
drooping heavy under your eyes.

Don't think about the number of people you could call
to discuss these negative ideations with.
Don't tell yourself nobody cares.
Don't remember how your ex-girlfriend knew
exactly how to make you feel small enough
to keep under her thumb for so long.
Don't remember the name-calling by bullies in school
or how you never fit in anywhere,
not even your own suffocating husk.

Don't think about how you will do it.
How it can't be a rope because of the history of lynching.
Also how you don't want to leave a mess
you've already felt like such a burden
so a gun or knife are out of the question.
Don't think about your fear of heights
how that must be why you are bad at building bridges.
Don't decide on pills so you can quietly disappear
from this world to the next, inconspicuous as always.

Don't think about the suit your mother will pick out for the service.
Don't think about which sister will cry the loudest
or how many times people will ask your brother.
*Why didn't he say something?* If I had only known.

Don't think about escaping the despair,
abuse claws its way out of your memories,
all you want to leave behind,
your body going numb.

There is something I beg you to do.

Wait.

Wait to see at least one more sapphire sunrise,
Wait to hear the infectious laughter of one more friend
Wait, taste one more bowl of holiday gumbo
Wait to smell one more lover's rose perfume
Wait to feel one more homie's bear hug

Wait until the day God calls you home.

# Sandprints

by Romaine Washington

the girl felt like a mound of brown sand in the middle of the white kitchen floor
when Momma glared at the girl / felt like she needed
to be swept up in a dustpan          and thrown away

her Momma never said she wanted
                    to throw the girl away
Momma wasn't yelling
                    at her in fierce hatred
wasn't casting a spell
                    to make her disappear
wasn't murdering her

wasn't burning off her hair
                    there was still enough to brush
wasn't burdened by her presence
                    as long as the girl stayed out of momma's way

Momma didn't despise
          the girl for taking up her time          but She used to dream...
Momma didn't wish          the girl did not exist          but She grumbled it when tired
Momma didn't wish          the girl was invisible          but She sighed it when lonely

and the girl did not stand for it
she was angry          a fierce pulsating in her fists
her hands began to swirl
                    and the heat of the energy
                    traveled up her arms
                    to her shoulders
                    down through her stomach
                    down to her feet
shod in white socks with lace trim
and black hot shiny patent leather shoes
                    the girl stomped
                    the earth absorbed her flames

the girl seared through the white linoleum floor
and everywhere the girl stepped became grey putty
and when the girl lifted her foot          the impression became a sandprint
                    the girl ran around the kitchen
                              up the walls

on the ceiling
and with each step
she was disintegrating into sand
until she came back to the same spot
she was standing in
when Momma shoved her
with eyes squinting hate

and the sand    that was a ghost of the girl
swirling around the house
came back together    grain-by-grain
she returned to that spot
glared back at Momma
who morphed into a colander
with long-slender-fingered hands
Momma scooped the girl up
and grains drained into days
and sighs with Momma
strained and raved into months with Mom
coagulated into mounds
of gifts and scuffles
of years with Mother

no longer a child

away from Mother    she still felt gray-rage-grit
grabbed a dustpan    went to therapy
grain by grain retraced her steps
to the middle of the white kitchen floor

now, a Tall Brown Woman
She faces her Mother
in the mirror
and says,
*I am here*
*to heal us*

# Internal Struggle for Life: Discussion Questions

Use these questions to spark conversation about the poems, stories, and essays in this section.

## One Hundred Minutes

by Brandon Allen

1. Are you surprised by the number of teens who commit suicide? How does the poet create a sense of urgency? What suggestions does he have for helping teens?

2. Are teens the only people in a crisis? Talk about other groups that you feel might be at risk and what strategies and provisions can we personally, and as a society, make for them.

---

## Long as Memory

by Chris TPG Green

1. In the previous poem, we were confronted by the crisis of teen suicides. In this poem we have a personal experience of loss. It doesn't sound like he knew the student well, but he went to school with him and cared about him, even from afar. This person experiences the loss on an intimate level. When someone takes their own life, it not only impacts immediate friends and family but also carries a ripple effect. Refer back to the poem, *The Five Stages* by Dr. Ahliah Sharp in the Mind/Body Wisdom section. What are some ways we can create self-care in the midst of tragedy, even as a community member?

---

## How are You

by Davian Chester

1. In the image, there are two people; one person says to the other person, "How are you? I truly want to know." Why do you think he had to reassure the person? When was the last time you asked someone how they were doing and encouraged an honest response? When was the last time someone asked you? What would you do if someone were in crisis?

## Break the Piñata on Timothy Street

Mario Tahi Lathan

1. Who is the piñata and what are some of the things he goes through?
2. What saves him?
3. What strategies do you use when you feel you are approaching your breaking point?

---

## I am a Romantasy Rewriting Herself

by Camille Hernandez

1. What are the different factors that aggravated the speaker's suicidal ideations?
2. Why doesn't the speaker want to leave a suicide note?
3. At the conclusion of this piece, are you concerned for the speaker's safety? What would you say to the speaker, and what steps do you think she could take to shift things away from the ideations?

---

## Death Still Checks in on Me

by Matthew E. Henry

1. How does the theme in this poem complement the theme in *I am a Romantasy Rewriting Herself* by Camille Hernandez? What are the differences?

---

## Sum Up a Day Compiled of Single Steps

by Eric DeVaughnn

1. One day at a time - one step at a time. What would you say to the speaker to validate his efforts, and what would you say to encourage him further on the quest for joy in living?

## ~~The Real Monster Is Never~~ Being Able to Place the Sound of

by Jordan Franklin

1. What does the speaker do in this poem to move to a place of joy in living?

---

## Suffocating Husk

by James Coats

1. In this poem, the poet is speaking to a person and pleading with him to not dwell on the negative moments and events in his life, but to wait for the possible good and see what life holds in store. While the poem is geared toward a person with specific life experiences, it could serve as a template for your own life's journey or to encourage someone in crisis. Reflect on the various ways you could "wait" until things get better.

2. You could use this poem as a template to write your own poem, substituting positive experiences and memories for negative ones.

---

## Sandprints

by Romaine Washington

1. Reread the poem and change the pronouns (boy/he/him or they/them). Does it matter if you change the pronouns? Do the events and emotions carry the same weight?

2. From the descriptions in the poem, what do you think are some of the girl's triggers?

3. What does the sand represent?

4. *Micro traumas are defined as* subtle, repetitive, or seemingly insignificant incidents that cause emotional or physical harm over time. *Psychological/Emotional key aspects*: Small, repetitive interactions that erode mental health. Examples include "little murders" (insults hidden in jokes), being ignored... Do you think the girl experienced microtraumas? What do you think her healing journey would look like?

# Resources

# *OCP Disorder References

A., Tony. "The Laundry List." Adult Children of Alcoholics® & Dysfunctional Families World Service Organization, https://adultchildren.org/literature/laundry-list/. Accessed 1 Aug. 2025.

Berman, Carole. "8 Tips on How to Recognize Someone with Obsessive-Compulsive Personality Disorder." *HuffPost*, Buzzfeed, 27 Nov. 2014, https://www.huffpost.com/entry/obsessive-compulsive-personality-disorder_b_5816816. Accessed 17 June 2025.

Kelly, Owen. "OCPD vs. OCD: What's the Difference?" Very Well Mind, 25 June 2024, https://www.verywellmind.com/ocd-vs-obsessive-compulsive-personality-disorder-2510584.

MD Searchlight Team. "Obsessive-Compulsive Personality Disorder." MD Searchlight, 8 July 2024, https://mdsearchlight.com/mental-health/obsessive-compulsive-personality-disorder/. Accessed 17 June 2025.

"Obsessive-Compulsive Personality Disorder (Deep Dive) - Chapter 1." Psychology in Seattle, hosted by Dr. Kirk Honda, Patreon, 17 Jan. 2022, Patreon app.

"Obsessive-Compulsive Personality Disorder (Deep Dive) - Chapter 3." Psychology in Seattle, hosted by Dr. Kirk Honda, Patreon, 21 Jan. 2022, Patreon app.

"Obsessive-Compulsive Personality Disorder (Deep Dive) - Chapter 2." Psychology in Seattle, hosted by Dr. Kirk Honda, Patreon, 19 Jan. 2022, Patreon app.

Obsessive-Compulsive Personality Disorder (OCPD)." Out of the FOG, https://outofthefog.website/personality-disorders-1/2015/12/6/obsessive-compulsive-personality-disorder-ocpd. Accessed 17 June 2025.

Rizvi, Abid, and Tyler J. Torrico. "Obsessive-Compulsive Personality Disorder." *StatPearls* [Internet], Treasure Island (FL): StatPearls Publishing; Jan. 2025, 28 Oct. 2023. *National Library of Medicine*, https://www.ncbi.nlm.nih.gov/books/NBK597372/.

Rossignol, Darryl. "What Are Personality Disorders?" The OCPD Foundation, 1 Mar. 2024, https://www.ocpd.org/personality-disorders. Accessed 17 June 2025.

—. "What Is OCPD?" The OCPD Foundation, 3 Mar. 2024, https://www.ocpd.org/what-is-ocpd. Accessed 17 June 2025.

Rothenberg, Albert. "Is Obsessive-Compulsive Personality Disorder a Problem?" Psychology Today, Sussex Publishers, 23 Aug. 2018, https://www.psychologytoday.com/us/blog/creative-explorations/201808/is-obsessive-compulsive-personality-disorder-problem. Accessed 17 June 2025.

Spett, Milton. "Obsessive-Compulsive Personality: The Overlooked Diagnosis." The OCPD Foundation, https://www.ocpd.org/articles/obsessive-compulsive-personality-the-overlooked-diagnosis. Accessed 3 June 2025.

T., Buddy. "Characteristics of Adult Children of Alcoholics." *Verywell Mind*, 28 Apr. 2024https://www.verywellmind.com/common-traits-of-adult-children-of-alcoholics-66 557. Accessed 31 Mar. 2025.

# Sources

**Introduction**

Akkas, Farzana & Corr, Allison. "Black Adolescent Suicide Rate Reveals Urgent Need to Address Mental Health Care Barriers." Cultural competency in health care, expanded use of screening tools, and more research on risk factors could help address increase among this demographic group. *The Pew Charitable Trusts*. 22 April, 2024. https://www.pew.org/en/research-and-analysis/articles/2024/04/22/black-adolescent-suicide-rate-reveals-urgent-need-to-address-mental-health-care-barriers

Bartlett, Steven. "Trevor Noah: My Depression was linked to ADHD! Why I left the Daily Show!" *The Diary of a CEO*. Podcast. 16 Oct. 2024 https://podcasts.apple.com/us/podcast/trevor-noah-my-depression-was-linked-to-adhd-why-i/id1291423644?i=1000673396240

Cartwright, Samuel A. "Report On The Diseases and Physical Peculiarities Of The Negro race." *The New Orleans Medical and Surgical Journal*. 1851.

Etienne, Vanessa. "Taraji P. Henson Talks Breaking the 'Cycle of Suffering' with Mental Health: 'Vulnerability Is Your Strength'." *People Magazine*. 09 May 2024. https://people.com/taraji-p-henson-talks-breaking-the-cycle-of-suffering-with-mental-health-8646048

Kallingal, Mallika "Simone Biles opens up about her mental health post-Olympics: 'I'm still scared to do gymnastics'." *CNN Sports*. 22 Oct. 2021. https://www.cnn.com/2021/10/22/sport/simone-biles-gymnastics-spt/index.html

Lane. Christopher. "How Schizophrenia Became a Black Disease: An Interview With Jonathan Metzl." *Psychology Today*. 05 May 2010. https://www.psychologytoday.com/us/blog/side-effects/201005/how-schizophrenia-became-black-disease-interview-jonathan-metzl

***Faith and Mental Health***

***Neurodivergent*** by Jay Writes

Quinn, Kimberly. The 4 Core Traits of ADHD, Explained. Understanding can be a catalyst for positive change. *Psychology Today*. 24 July 2021. https://www.psychologytoday.com/us/blog/optimized/202107/the-4-core-traits-adhd-explained

***Resurrection*** by Alexander James, ***Depression*** by Lydia Theon Ware i, ***Chaos*** by Marcus Thompson, and ***What the Preacher Said*** by Anjetta (Anjie) Williams

Winch, Guy. "The Important Difference Between Sadness and Depression... and why so many get it wrong." *Psychology Today*. 02, Oct. 2015. https://www.psychologytoday.com/us/blog/the-squeaky-wheel/201510/the-important-difference-between-sadness-and-depression

***Mind and Body Wisdom***

Hersey, Tricia. Rest is Resistance: *A Manifesto*. Little, Brown Spark, 2022.

***She Lives Always Seeking the Silver Lining***

National Institute of Mental Health (NIMH): NIMH provides resources on managing mental health in the context of chronic illness. Their publication on chronic illness and mental health provides insights into recognizing and treating mental health conditions that may arise from living with chronic diseases like sickle cell disease. "Chronic Illness and Mental Health: Recognizing and Treating." https://www.nimh.nih.gov/health/publications/chronic-illness-mental-health

National Library of Medicine (NLM / PMC): NLM provides access to scientific literature."Mental Health Challenges associated with Sickle Cell Disease and Strategies to Address Them: Reflections from a Community Input Panel." 31, Dec. 2025. https://pmc.ncbi.nlm.nih.gov/articles/PMC12752931/

# Resources

Black Emotional and Mental health Collective. (BEAM). The Black Emotional and Mental Health Collective (BEAM) is a national 501c3organization that trains, funds, holds healing space and resources an international network of therapists, wellness practitioners, healing justice efforts and grassroots wellness initiatives to transform and support the well being and mental health of our most marginalized communities. https://beam.community/

Healthy Heritage Movement: Broken Crayons Still Color. Created to target and address health disparities within the African American community, Healthy Heritage Movement focuses on the wellbeing of African Americans through health education, policy change, and community outreach. https://healthyheritage.org/about-the-movement/

National Alliance on Mental Illness (NAMI): NAMI is a nationwide, grassroots mental health organization. NAMI offers educational programs, advocates for individuals and families affected by mental illness, and operates a toll-free helpline. https://www.nami.org/

The National Domestic Violence Hotline 800-799-7233 or Text START to 88788. https://www.thehotline.org/get-help/

Suicide Prevention Hotline: The 988 Lifeline provides 24/7, free and confidential support for people in distress

# Contributors

**Brandon Allen** is a poet, speaker, and nonprofit leader who transforms storytelling into a vehicle for healing and empowerment. A survivor of abuse, he uses his journey to inspire authenticity and emotional resilience. As the Founder and Executive Director of Youth Writers Camp Inc., he helps students explore creative writing, mental health, and publishing. Brandon's voice has been featured at TEDx Compton Blvd, Netflix, and Amazon. He is committed to creating spaces where young people feel seen, confident, and capable of shaping their future.

**Keisha-Gaye Anderson** is an award-winning poet, artist, and author of three poetry collections: *A Spell for Living, Everything Is Necessary,* and *Gathering the Waters.* Her writing has been widely published in outlets like the *Academy of American Poets, Caribbean Writer, Prairie Schooner, Langston Hughes Review, Peregrine, SX Salon*, and others. Keisha holds an MFA in Creative Writing from The City College, CUNY, and a BA from Syracuse University, Newhouse School. Learn more at www.keishagaye.ink.

**Violeta Antonette** is a mother, wife, mental health professional, and aspirational contemplative writer based in Detroit, MI. She runs a therapy practice that focuses on helping Black women heal from complex trauma and racial stress. One of her favorite pastimes is watching comedy specials with unique perspectives on the political state of the world. Learn more about her at www.violeta-emdr.com.

**Stephani Maari Booker** is surviving the fire, plague, and wrath of 2020s Minneapolis, MN, by creating works for the page and the stage in which she wrestles with her multiple marginalized identities: African American, lesbian, lower-class, and disabled. She is a recipient of a 2024 McKnight Fellowship for Writers Administered by the Loft and a 2024 Minnesota State Arts Board Creative Individuals Grant. For more information about Stephani's work, go to www.athenapersephoni.com.

**Akilah Brown** is an award-winning professor, blogger, and multi-genre storyteller who was a 2023 writing fellow for the Joshua Tree Highlands Artist Residency and a past scholarship recipient for the Rocaberti Writers' Retreat. Originally from Bladensburg, MD, she now lives and writes in Los Angeles, CA. Learn more about her at theakilahbrown.com

**Pastor Samuel J. Casey, M.A.,** is the Senior Founding Shepherd of New Life Christian Church of Fontana and the Executive Director of Congregations Organized for Prophetic Engagement (C.O.P.E.). A faith-rooted organizer, preacher, and community leader, Pastor Casey is devoted to bridging faith and justice, empowering believers to live with courage, compassion, and conviction in pursuit of holistic transformation spiritually, mentally, and socially.

**Pastor Tamika Casey** is an assistant pastor, educator, author, and equity leader committed to empowering individuals and communities through faith, education, and service. She serves in district-level leadership, supporting culturally responsive practices and improved outcomes for African American students. Her work is rooted in helping people heal, grow, and walk boldly in purpose.

**Davian Chester** is an artist and storyteller known for *Real Toons*, a comic series that explores Black experiences with humor and honesty. His work seamlessly blends activism, culture, and everyday life to spark meaningful conversations.

**James Coats** is an award-winning author, poet, and educator from Southern California. You can take a poetry workshop with him through his organization, Lift Our Voices Education, which hosts an award-winning workshop monthly called Be the Change: Social Justice Writing Workshop. He's a 2023 Poetry Pushcart Prize nominee.

**Naysha Coker** is a restorative, empathic writer whose work explores identity through the lens of mental health. Rooted in faith, her collection *Piece by Peace* blends therapeutic insight with radical acceptance and grace— inviting readers to see wholeness as an inseparable part of holistic health.

**Nia Crawford** is an instructor who writes from Baltimore and Philadelphia and has taught writing to middle schoolers and college students for over 20 years. She's been published in *Ink Nest Poetry, BODY, Necessary Fiction*, and *Killens Review of Arts and Letters*. Nia is also a real estate agent, and she enjoys volunteering and supporting community-based organizations.

**Eric DeVaughnn** is a father and poet. He has hosted open mics, is the founder of innateDIVINITYbooks, has a few self-published collections, and is a recurring judge for Poetry Out Loud. Eric teaches elementary physical education in San Bernardino, California. All his poems are cracked teeth, dusky yellow and receding gum line lying limp on waxy, bright white paper, speckled red.

**Angelique DeVonish** is a poet, writer, orator, and visual artist who hails from The Bronx, NY, by way of Bowie, Maryland. As a Black American, lesbian, spiritualist, Angelique's work showcases her intersectionality, and how her unique navigation of life challenges ideas around identity, autonomy, and self-empowerment.

**Nicole J. Evans** (she/her) is a Black woman, born and reared in Los Angeles. 2024 James Kirkwood Prize nominee who creates fiction, creative nonfiction, and poetry. Pre-Matriarch, Black sheep, vision alchemist, generational curse breaker, generational blessing manifester, dream catcher, tale weaver, aspiring griot, empath, latent gardener, inherent beautician, poet by heart, writer by revelation, and singer of her own songs. IG @itsnicolejeanine, email njevanswrites@gmail.com

**Tona Farlow** is a Licensed Marriage and Family Therapist with extensive experience helping individuals, couples, and families overcome life's challenges. Her client-centered, solution-focused approach empowers clients to set meaningful goals and develop practical strategies for healing and growth. She specializes in anxiety, depression, trauma, and substance abuse, and is EMDR certified. Passionate about working with children and teens, she provides a compassionate, supportive space where clients feel heard, understood, and empowered to thrive.

**Angela M. Franklin** is an author, poet, essayist, documentarian, and visual artist from Los Angeles, California. She holds an MFA from Antioch University. Social justice issues and helping others find their voice are among her passions. Her work has appeared in a variety of anthologies. She is currently working on a memoir about growing up in Los Angeles and a book of poetry about her brother's struggle with mental illness and eventual death because of it.

**Jordan E. Franklin** hails from Brooklyn, NY. She is the author of the poetry collection, *when the signals come home* (Switchback Books), and the chapbook, *boys in the electric age* (Tolsun Books). Her work has appeared in *Crab Orchard Review, Luna Luna Magazine, Hanging Loose Press, SWWIM, Torch Literary Arts, Obsidian,* and *elsewhere.*

**Ginger M. Galloway** (author/poet) wishes that treating mental illness were as common as treating the common cold. It should not carry a cloak of shame or embarrassment.Ginger's work can be found in *These Black Bodies Are... A Blacklandia Anthology* (Inlandia) and *Saltwater* (Jamii Publishing). Find her other books on Amazon.

**April Gardner** is a child of God, a daughter, a sister, and an auntie. She has been called to be an educator and has walked in her calling diligently and faithfully. She also has a creative side that allows her to speak about her family, feelings, and truth in the form of a short story or letter.

**Beverly George** is a poet who taught music/chorus in Sumter School District, S.C., for 22 years. In 2022, her first chapbook, *First Light*, was published, followed by *Amazing Grace*, in 2024. Her work can be found in the *Petigru Review*, 2024, and in the *Tuskegee Review* Issue 3, 2024, and *S.C. Bards Anthology* 2023 - 2025.

**Chris TPG Green** is now 39 years old, still trying to bend his humanity into poems, still seeking the questions more than answers. TPG uses his faith, his background, and his perception to try to discover poetry beyond this world's walls.

**Velvet Gunn** is a Chicago-born, multi-disciplinary artist, author, & entrepreneur. Her work sits at an intersection between art, wellness, and spirituality. Her mission is to create innovative, thought-provoking art and experiences that act as portals for connection and expanded awareness. Through writing and production, Velvet curates pieces to challenge perspective, foster belonging, and build community. More at www.byvelvetgunn.com

**George Hammons** lives and writes poetry in Southern California. He is the author of two chapbooks: *Hungry to Bed / Love Poems* (Arroyo Seco Press) and *Witness* (Picture Show Press). Known for his accessible yet thought-provoking style, George explores themes of social justice, love, and parenting.

**Monique Reneé Harris** was born an African American woman with spastic cerebral palsy. Her poetry and essays have been published in *DailyHaiga, Sun Magazine, Magnets & Ladders, Wordgathering, URevolution, Dryland, Seeing Beyond the Surface,* and *Wordpeace*. *Spoonie Press* nominated her essay "Aging with Spastic Cerebral Palsy" for the 2022 Best of the Net Award. In 2019, she self-published a poetry and art book titled *Strength and Tragedy: The Mystery of the Blue Lady.*

**Beverly Head** is the author of *Walking North*, winner of the Naomi Long Madgett Poetry Award.

**Camille Hernandez** (she/her) is a Black and Filipina poet, mother, organizer, and Anaheim's 2023-2025 Poet Laureate. Equipped by her matriarchal cultures and motherhood journey, Camille writes and leads from the fluid depths of tenderness, protection, and intuition. She authored the books *Motherlands* (Finishing Line Press) and *The Hero and the Whore* (Westminster John Knox Press). Her website is www.camillehernandez.com

**Matthew E. Henry** (MEH) is an educator, editor, essayist, and the author of seven poetry collections, including the forthcoming *Promises to Keep* (Wayfarer Books, 2026). Editor-in-chief of *The Weight Journal* and nonfiction editor at *Porcupine Literary*, MEH earned an MFA yet continued to spend money he didn't have completing an MA in theology and a PhD in education. He writes about education, race, religion, and burning oppressive systems to the ground at www.MEHPoeting.com.

**Dana I. Hunter** is a top poet in the NAMI NJ: Dara Axelrod Expressive Arts Poetry Contest. Her Micro-Chapbook *Excavating a Relationship* is published by Bottlecap Press. She has been featured in Heather Stivison's Ekphrasis! at Pleiades Gallery in NYC; published in *The Decolonial Passage Literary Magazine, Songs or Ertez, The Journal of Undiscovered Poets, table/FEAST Literary Magazine,* and *Open Minds Quarterly*. Dana advocates for the end of stigma against mental illness through her writing.

**Alexander James** is a poet, pastor, and truth-teller from South Los Angeles whose work bridges faith, honesty, and the human experience. A 2022 Addy and Webby Award recipient, he's shared his voice from Inglewood to Israel, using poetry as a mirror and medicine. Through his company, Be Honest, Alexander creates spaces where vulnerability becomes strength and truth leads to freedom. His debut poetry collection, *Just Be Honest*, invites readers into courageous self-reflection.

**Tiara Jones** is a Limitation Liberation coach from Detroit, rooting for everybody Black. She's learning to hate her life less by expressing herself more. Writing is her latest ADHD obsession and her favorite form of resistance. The contents of her Notes app are finally going public.

**Justin C. Key** is a practicing psychiatrist and a speculative fiction writer. He is the author of the story collection *The World Wasn't Ready for You*, and the sci-fi thriller *The Hospital at the End of the World*. His stories have appeared in the *Magazine of Fantasy & Science Fiction, Strange Horizons, Lightspeed,* and on Tor.com. He completed his residency in psychiatry at UCLA and lives in Los Angeles with his wife and three children.

**Reverie Koniecki** is a Black writer and educator living in Dallas, Texas. Her work has appeared in *Callaloo, Guernica, Post Road*, and other places. She is the author of chapbooks —*to the god of sore feet and bad backs* (Finishing Line Press) and *The Wars That Steer Us* (Mouthfeel Press).

**Mario Tahi Lathan** is a native of Cincinnati, Ohio, holding an MFA in Film from Howard University. An award-winning filmmaker, writer, and always a dreamer, he explores the beauty of the Black experience through an improvised jazz aesthetic. His eternal blessing lies in fatherhood to William and Sofia.

**Stephanie Liggins** is a wife, mother, proud grandmother, retired teacher, and an ordained minister of the Gospel. After receiving a certificate in creative writing in 1985, she stopped writing. But the stories continue to cry out, desperate to be heard. So, she has picked up her pen again. Let's see where the spirit leads.

**Ipyani Lockert** is a Photographer of Engaging Captures, Caught: A photography service of MotivationalRealizations.com

**Sheila Louise Bennett Marchbanks**, MBA, aka **She-She**, is a sojourner focused on her family, Biblical faith, and fulfilling service. She's an avid reader, audiobook fan, lifelong learner, eager world globe trotter, dedicated succulent gardener, and grateful grandmother extraordinaire. As a retired Aerospace Executive, Sheila has parlayed her professional expertise into being a dedicated Sickle Cell Disease advisor and ambassador, active community leader, advocate, educator, and partner. Her Senior Years are Sweet Years.

**Amaya Marshall** is a sixteen-year-old writer who is based in Southern California. She focuses on writing short stories and essays that relate to feminism and the Black experience. She has been writing fiction and non-fiction privately for over four years. Outside of writing, she commits to social justice and activist work in her community by donating to women's shelters, raising awareness on domestic violence, and sexual assault. She is currently working on her first novella.

**Brittany Miles** writes lyrical fiction and essays exploring family, motherhood, and mental health. Her emotionally resonant work has appeared in *Newsweek, Business Insider, The Seattle Times, Open Secrets, Blood+Honey, MUTHA Magazine,* and is forthcoming in *Tir Literary Magazine.*

**Devin Mitchell** has been writing poetry since he was thirteen, and he is now an alumnus of California State University, San Bernardino. He is currently an MSW student at Simmons University. This is his second publication with Blacklandia, and he hopes it resonates with the reader.

**Kache' Attyana Mumford** is a poet, playwright, and drama therapist whose work examines silence, healing, and inherited memory within Black womanhood. Her poems appear or are forthcoming in *Allium, Vermilion, Cathexis Northwest Press, Budin: The McNeese Review,* and *The Closed Eyes Open.* She was a finalist for the Tennessee Williams & New Orleans Literary Festival Poetry Award and is the 2025 recipient of Emory University's African American History & Culture Research Award.

**Carmen Estela Kennedy Saleh** is a writer and a perennial learner who is as at home in class discussions as she is planted behind a good book. She has articles in the *Themis and Acacia* journals, respectively. She was honored with a James D. Phelan Literary Award and a Solas Award for Culture and Ideas. And, in 2023, she debuted *A Love Letter*, a bestseller in May and June of that same year.
carmenestelakennedysaleh.com

**Mervyn Seivwright** writes to balance social consciousness & poetry craft for humane growth. He is Jamaican, born in England. He has appeared in *AGNI, African American Review, Salamander Magazine, Poetry.online*, & 85 other journals across 13 countries. He is the 2024 Marvin E. Williams Literary Prize winner & a 2021/2023 Pushcart Nominee. His collection is "Stick, Hook, and a Pile of Yarn," Broken Sleep Books.

**Dr. Ahliah Sharp** was born and raised in the Inland Empire with a childhood dream of becoming a child psychologist. She eventually switched to both clinical and industrial-organizational psychology, respectively. Her passion is to help others through her words, wisdom, and worship. Mental health is her passion, and educating others about it is her purpose.

**Tiffany Smalls** received her BA in Creative Writing from SUNY Potsdam and spent most of her life in Rome, NY. Currently residing in Seattle, WA, she divides her time between being an executive assistant and making handcrafted jewelry. Her work has appeared in publications by *Shō Poetry Journal, Quarter Press, BLF Press, Paragon Press, Firewords Magazine, Beatific Magazine, Coffin Bell Journal,* and *Genre: Urban Art,* amongst others.

**Marcus Thompson** has an 18-year career in law enforcement and a passion for protecting those who need it. He found his escape from the difficult times life presents by pouring his heart and soul into his poetry. He's been writing for most of his life and loves challenging himself to reach new depths in his creativity. In addition, he is a proud father of two beautiful daughters.

**Lydia F. Theon Ware i** writes poetry for the forgotten. She has been published in two issues of *Cholla Needles* anthologies. She dances and choreographs for the Lord. Her dreams are to write plays for broken women. She loves science fiction and horror stories.

**Jasmine Vallejo-Love** is a disabled Afro-Puerto Rican American poet and writer living in Los Angeles. Her poetry and essays engage with social issues such as mental illness, domestic violence, addiction, and sexual assault. A Diana Woods Memorial Award finalist, 2025 Lambda Literary Emerging LGBTQ Voices Fellow, and selected for PEN America's Emerging Voices workshop, her work has been anthologized and appears in journals such as *Lunch Ticket* and *Cholla Needles*. Find her on Instagram @CafecitoWithJas

**Anjetta (Anjie) Williams-Brown** is a Tennessee State University retiree after 22 years of service. She self-published her first poetry book in 2022. She hosts three open mic poetry programs, one author/artist spotlight program, and one talk show. She has poems in anthologies and magazines.

**Sharon M. Williams** is an author, poet, and teacher in the Greater Los Angeles area. She has two poetry collections, *Two Truths Wise* (2011) and *Dark Days Light* (2022). She also enjoys fostering a vibrant writing community and inspiring others across all genres to share their stories.

**Quan Williams** is a director at a community-based organization in the Inland Empire Region of California. She has earned several academic degrees, including a bachelor's degree in Pan-African Studies: Arts and Literature from California State University Northridge. Quan is a member of Delta Sigma Theta Sorority, Inc., and embraces community service as a lifetime commitment. Aside from work, Quan enjoys being an auntie, sports, comedy, and music.

**André Le Mont Wilson** was born in Los Angeles, the son of the writer Jessie Lee Dawson-Wilson. After she died in 2012, his brother discovered her unpublished essay, "After the Sun Went Down," inside a kitchen closet dresser. The winner of the 2022 Newfound Prose Prize for his chapbook *The Hauntings*, Wilson's published works include the "A Walk with Mom" essay about his mother in *These Bodies Are . . . A Blacklandia Anthology.*

**Ellen June Wright** is an American writer with British and Caribbean roots. Her work has been published in *Caribbean Writer, Obsidian, POETRY Magazine*, and is forthcoming in *The American Poetry Review.*

**Jonathan Ezemba**, also known as **Jay Writes**, is an author, multidisciplinary performing artist, and event curator. Jonathan is an advocate for liberation through self and collective expression. He verbally illustrates the beauty within the community, struggles with identity, and reflects on his own experiences and the world at large. Writes curates, and hosts open mics, writing workshops, jam sessions, and poetry slams with Rhythms and Poetry at the only black-owned art gallery in Austin, RichesArt Gallery.

**Alora Young** is the 5th Youth Poet Laureate of the Southern United States. Her book *Walking Gentry Home* (Penguin Random House) was named the debut of the year by The Nashville Scene, received a starred review in Kirkus, was nominated for a Goodreads Choice Award, and was a best seller on Amazon. She was a Presidential Scholar of the Arts, a 2X TEDx speaker. and a Davidson "Youth Genius Grant" Fellow. She is a Best Young Actress award winner, as well as a poet, and has performed her poetry on CNN, CBS, TIME, and many other channels.

**Angelique Zobitz** (she/her/hers) is the author of *Seraphim* (CavanKerry Press) and the chapbooks *Love Letters to The Revolution* (American Poetry Journal) and *Burn Down Your House* from Milk & Cake Press. Her work appears in *The Journal, About Place, Penn Review, Sugar House Review, Obsidian: Literature & Arts of the African Diaspora*, and many others. She can be found at www.angeliquezobitz.com and on Instagram: @angeliquezobitz

# About the Editor

Romaine Washington is an Inland Empire native, the editor of *These Black Bodies Are... A Blacklandia Anthology*, and a guest editor of the literary journal, Cholla Needles issues 102 and 88. Washington is the author of two poetry books, *Purgatory Has an Address* and *Sirens in Her Belly*, and is a twice-nominated Pushcart Prize poet whose work has also been nominated for Best of the Net. She is a graduate fellow of The Water Hole and Inland Area Writing Project, UC Riverside. A late-in-life diagnosis of ADHD inspired Washington to curate a Black anthology to help break stigma and build supportive conversations about mental illness and wellness. To find out more, visit her website at: www.romainewashington.com.

# About Blacklandia

Inlandia Institute's Blacklandia Events Series was initiated in 2020 in response to the murder of George Floyd at the hands of the police on May 25 of that year. As an organization centered around the power of words, one that values speaking up, and speaking out, Inlandia made a renewed and public commitment to providing a space for people in the Black community to come together, and from that arose a Black-led Black voices steering committee, and a new series of events, Blacklandia.

# Acknowledgments

Angela M. Franklin, thank you for your prayers and friendship, your dedicated research and advice, and your artistic and creative support; without your help, this anthology would be incomplete.

Thank you to my Blacklandia family, Ginger Galloway, James Coats, Lydia Theon Ware i, Sebraé Harris, Lisa Henry, Nikia Chaney, Richard Allen May III, Ipyani Lockert, and Alex Avila. I have enjoyed attending events, being on panel talks, and learning from and growing with you. Thank you for your many kindnesses, hugs, writing bonds, and encouragement.

Inlandia: Cati Porter, thank you for believing in me and for the opportunity to curate and edit *These Black Bodies Are... A Blacklandia Anthology* and for access to the various reading venues that helped the anthology build community. The successful completion of that project gave me the confidence to curate and edit *88 Unashamed Black Mental Health Stories*. Thank you for your friendship and support through this process. Janine Pourroy-Gamblin, thank you for the many photos and conversations, for your kindness, your insight, support, and encouragement. Thank you, Juanita Mantz, for your support and friendship. Mckenna Deluca-Martinez and the Board of Directors thank you for your faith in and funding of this project.

Women Who Submit, thank you for your consistent practice of writing and submitting, which has been a constant source of encouragement, validation, and resilience. I love that some members have submitted to and are included in this collection.

Thank you to the people who privately shared stories with me, but for one reason or another, were unable to include them in this collection. I treasure your trust. Thank you to everyone who contributed to this collection. Your openness and vulnerability, your creativity and courage, your voice and vision are healing.

www.ingramcontent.com/pod-product-compliance
Lightning Source LLC
LaVergne TN
LVHW050617100826
845148LV00011B/1632

* 9 7 8 1 7 3 4 4 9 7 7 2 4 *